The Labrador Retriever Dog Bible

2 in 1

Everything You Need To Know About Choosing, Raising, Training, And Caring Your Labrador From Puppyhood To Senior Years

Kimberly Lawrence

Copyright 2019 © Kimberly Lawrence

All rights reserved.

No part of this guide may be reproduced in any form without permission in writing from the publisher except in the case of review.

Legal & Disclaimer

The following document is reproduced below with the goal of providing information that is as accurate and reliable as possible.

This declaration is deemed fair and valid by both the American Bar Association and the Committee of Publishers Association and is legally binding throughout the United States.

Furthermore, the transmission, duplication or reproduction of any of the following work including specific information will be considered an illegal act irrespective of if it is done electronically or in print. This extends to creating a secondary or tertiary copy of the work or a recorded copy and is only allowed with an express written consent from the Publisher. All additional right reserved.

The information in the following pages is broadly considered to be a truthful and accurate account of facts, and as such any inattention, use or misuse of the information in question by the reader will render any resulting actions solely under their purview. There are no scenarios in which the publisher or the original author of this work can be in any fashion deemed liable for any hardship or damages that may befall them after undertaking information described herein.

Additionally, the information in the following pages is intended only for informational purposes and should thus be thought of as universal. As befitting its nature, it is presented without assurance regarding its prolonged validity or interim quality. Trademarks that are mentioned are done without written consent and can in no way be considered an endorsement from the trademark holder.

Table of Contents

Book 1:
The Labrador Retriever Handbook

The Complete Guide To Choosing, Training, And Caring Your Labrador For Keeping Your Companion Healthy, Happy, And Well-Behaved From Puppyhood To Senior Years

Introduction

This handbook provides essential information and helpful advice for all stages of life specific to Labrador retrievers. You'll find the pros and cons associated with the breed to help you make a sound decision when choosing a dog that suits your lifestyle. Initially, you will learn the origin of the breed and the behaviors associated with the original purpose for the dogs. By knowing the history and understanding the motivations behind the behavior of modern Labradors, you will know the level of commitment required to raise and care for a Labrador retriever.

The breed requires a great deal of time, space, exercise, and training, in addition to the recommended preventative and ongoing health care. In return, you'll have a spirited, loving companion that never runs short on personality. A Labrador can be many things to many different people, from a hunting buddy to a nightly protector sleeping at the foot of your child's bed. The breed has a sturdy, muscular build and a strong desire to please its owner. From bringing in a net of fish to catching a floppy Frisbee a dozen times in a row, a Lab will be happy to do the work.

There are many points to consider before making a definite decision, and the upcoming chapters will explain the extent of training, grooming, behavior concerns, and possible health issues known to surface specifically in Labrador retrievers.

Read on for more information on the traits of heredity, the importance of proper breeding, and potential challenges that can arise through the various stages of life. You'll gain an understanding of the amount of dedication and care it takes to help your puppy grow into a well-adjusted adult. You'll also learn what you can do to maintain health as your dog enters the senior years and beyond. There's something gained in every stage of life, and nothing quite like the memories made when you share your home with a Labrador.

List of Topics

The information in this book is arranged in a timeline that correlates with stages of life, from puppyhood through the senior years of a Labrador retriever. Each section provides information on both breed specific and general canine issues, including nutrition, training, and health.

Chapter 1 presents information on choosing a breeder, picking the right puppy from a litter, where not to shop for a puppy as well as puppy-proofing your home.

Chapter 2 will cover the various stages of training a Lab requires and training classes that are optional. This chapter will also have information for getting started with basic commands.

Chapter 3 presents information about nutrition and considerations for choosing the right food for your dog. There is also information about portion control and the optimal number of meals per day. The chapter then discusses health care and preventative medicine issues to help you make informed decisions about caring for your dog and protecting against disease and parasites.

Chapter 4 will give you advice, practices, and recommendations for keeping your dog clean, groomed, and clipped. You will also learn ways to keep shedding from becoming problematic and also methods to use to get your puppy used to all things grooming related.

Chapter 5 provides information on health issues and diseases that could potentially affect your dog. Specific information about increased risk that comes with aging is also included alongside descriptions of the most common canine diseases. Lastly, the final chapter gives you information about the choices pet owners have when faced with difficult end-of-life choices.

Origin of the Breed

The first lesson about America's top dog is an interesting and unexplained fact about the origin of the breed. The Labrador retriever doesn't come from Labrador. Their first home was in Newfoundland, Canada, where they helped fishermen retrieve not only nets of fish, but also ones that had escaped through the meshwork.

Their thick, short water-repellant coat worked well for waterfowl gaming pursuits, so the breed also partnered with duck hunters early on.

The first ancestral Labrador breeds began to develop as far back as the 1500s, but the good-natured dogs gained a major boost in popularity when discovered by British hunters in the early nineteenth century.

The traditional water dogs received additional favor on land as a retrieving gun dog when English aristocrats on sporting excursions in Canada took notice of the sturdy breed's exceptional skills. By the late 1800s, breeders in England had fine-tuned the standards of the breed and Labrador retrievers received recognition by both the English and American kennel clubs by 1917.

Purpose

The original hunting and sporting purpose of Labrador retrievers required the breed to be robust and high-spirited. Today, that results in a friendly, energetic pet that is ready to please, but also one that has a lot of energy to burn. Prospective pet owners should consider the high amount of exercise required to keep a Lab happy and healthy before committing to the breed. Aside from the obvious requirements, like food and water, the two major needs essential for a Lab are time with their owners and a lot of space to run, swim, and play.

The breed's high level of intelligence also sets the stage for boredom when a Lab doesn't receive sufficient tasks that stimulate the brain. An active, bored dog sets the stage for destructive behavior, so prospective owners should realistically evaluate their ability to provided adequate daily stimulation.

Standards

The combination of a friendly face and sturdy build sums up the basic appearance associated with America's most popular dog. But there are specific criteria the average Lab must meet to receive AKC recognition.

Labradors should weigh between 50 to 80 pounds, depending on gender, with females being on the lighter end of the scale. Similarly, male dogs will be taller, averaging 22.5 to 24.5 inches at the shoulder, while females range from 21.5 to 23.5 inches in height. A variance of half inch either way is grounds for disqualification.

Labradors are considered a medium-sized breed, but they have a stout muscular build that should be well defined and generally proportional, without excesses in any one area of the body.

The coat should be short and dense without any evidence of wave or curl. The only acceptable colors per standard are yellow, black, chocolate, and any variance or mix of colors would result in disqualification.

Feature	AKC Breed Standard
Weight	55–80 lbs.
Height	21.5–24.5 inches at shoulder
Coat	Thick, short, straight
Colors	Black, yellow, chocolate
Proportion	Short-coupled, no excess in any one area
Substance	Working condition, muscular
Note: Height and weight allowances vary according to gender.	

Choosing the Right Puppy for You

The most important information to consider before deciding to add a canine to your family involves research breed-specific characteristic that suits your lifestyle. For Labradors, the basic pros include a loving personality and a gentle temperament.

The cons involve space and exercise requirements, strong chewing instincts, and keeping the level of shedding under control.

Another consideration prospective Labrador owners face is deciding between a male or a female puppy. As far as gender, there are no definitive differences in disposition. All dogs, male and female, can be overly aggressive or excessively antisocial. The gender's role in personality is minuscule compared to the impact training and breeding have in forming a dog's temperament. More specific information on those topics will follow.

For now, there are some gender-specific facts that can help if you're indecisive.

Females versus Males

When it comes to training, female dogs may pick

up more readily on training only because they tend to mature sooner than their male counterparts.

Both genders of Labs typically have a high level of intelligence and a drive to please their owners. The only advantage of female puppies, training-wise, amounts to their ability to learn earlier than males of the same age.

When males catch up in maturity, the playing field levels out.

These procedures benefit the health of the dog and will also ensure that offspring don't end up a part of the population of animal shelters or one of the high numbers of pets that are euthanized each year. More specific information on spaying and neutering appears in upcoming chapters.

Temperament

The look of pure joy you see in a Labrador's expression demonstrates its true easy-going, fun-loving nature. The breed has a reputation for being tolerant of effervescent young children as well as other domestic animals.

This combination of mild-mannered characteristics has played a major role in moving the Labrador retriever to the top of the popularity chart in American.

One reason the breed makes suitable companions for families involves their origin. Labrador retrievers, of course, were bred to retrieve, and the job required a dog with a gentle bite that wouldn't damage the hunter's merchandise.

This gentleness carries forward into all other

encounters, including the domestic arena.

Exceptions

As with all breeds, there is no guarantee that these traits hold true across the board. There are many variables, such as breeding, environment, and level of training, that determine a dog's demeanor, and deficiencies could bring negative, even aggressive, behavior.

Fortunately, aggression and other undesirable qualities are not the typical traits of a healthy, well-bred, and well-cared-for Labrador.

What makes them unique?

What's one thing Labradors have in abundance? Personality. The breed received the lion's share of it. From the rambunctious, bumbling puppy that sometimes trips over its own feet, to the loyal and lively adult dog that sleeps at the foot of your child's bed, the breed has a humorously endearing character.

However, this friendly demeanor also translates into a pet that thrives on attention, to the point that not enough could result in undesirable behavior.

An active, friendly, and intelligent dog does not respond well to boredom, and destructive behavior is a typical response to too much downtime.

Prospective Lab owners need to evaluate the amount of time and attention their lifestyle realistically can dedicate to a pet with a high demand for exercise, training, and attention.

Basic Attributes of Labrador Retrievers

General Appearance	Muscular
Color	Black, yellow, or chocolate
Coat	Dense, short, straight coat
Temperament	Even-tempered and friendly
Trainability	Highly intelligent
Advantages	Friendly Good family companion Intelligent
Disadvantages	Sheds undercoat Strong chewing tendencies in youth High exercise and stimulation needs

The Lab will want to be an equal part of the family and won't be happy left alone. This will not be completely unavoidable, and understandably, so you will need to be proactive with finding ways to occupy your pup when you can't be there. You can find ideas about interactive toys in chapter 2.

In short, there are puzzle-style toys that have varying levels of difficulty, and food is usually the attraction. There are compartments for food that will take some work to extract.

In addition to time, you will need to include daily exercise in a consistent routine. Labs are built for action, and they need a regular amount of it to keep them happy and healthy. With all the energy they have been awarded by heritage, they will need an appropriate activity to expend it. If not given the opportunity to do what they were meant to do, your Lab could show his dissatisfaction by exhibiting bad behavior—mostly of the destructive type.

And Labs can create quite a mess when their energy is expended in the form of rebellious acts. Lab owners with busy schedules can attest to this fact. It's not uncommon when your intelligent and energetic ball of fur is left without entertainment, to come home to find quite of bit of redecorating has taken place in your absence. One average-sized Lab can easily rip couch cushion into bits—and in a very short time span. Lab owners have come home to find their Lab had spent the day reworking the wood on the baseboards in the living room. This activity mainly involved pulling the boards completely out of the wall.

Another Lab owner shared a story of when she left her six-month-old Lab shut in a bathroom while she ran some errands. When she returned home, her Lab met her at the door. When she went to investigate the way her Houdini escaped, she found that the entire bottom half of the bathroom door no longer existed.

The dogs don't do this type of destruction because they are mean-spirited. The situation is quite the opposite. They are highly social and have the drive to be around action and activity. And when they can't find either in their location, they do the best they can make their own.

The best correction for this type of behavior is two-fold. Find an activity where they expend energy prior to the time you need to leave them alone. Secondly, give then options for entertainment that are more appealing than wood and furniture. There are no training methods that will end this type of behavior. It's something Labradors do.

If you don't have time for exercise and activity provision, you could consider putting your dog in a form of childcare for canines. Doggy day care businesses started appearing in recent years in response to the needs of busy dog owners.

You can bring your Lab to one of these businesses every day during the work week or make single day drop-offs as needed. The daycares typically provide wide open space and a lot of structured activity to keep dogs entertained while owners make a living. Dogs are required to show proof of up-to-date vaccinations and need to be open to sharing the day with other dogs. When possible, the dogs are grouped according to size to avoid possible injuries from interactions toy breeds and the giants.

Most likely you will have options in your area to choose because of the growing popularity of this service. You will want to thoroughly investigate a business before choosing to leave your pup in their care.

The first and best way to get the scoop on the best daycares is to ask other dog owners. Word of mouth can prove most reliable. Suggestions can come from your vet or trainer, also. Despite raving reviews you might hear, you need to set up a tour of a facility. Most likely the business owner will prefer you come without your dog for this initial introduction.

While you're perusing the areas where your dog will be free to play, pay attention to cleanliness.

This includes any areas with strong odors both from pets and chemical cleaners. Neither is good for your puppy's health. Some facilities invest in pet-friendly cleaners that disinfect without adverse effects on the respiratory system.

Also, pay attention to the dogs that are present. Do they all look healthy? You don't what to expose your pup to potentially contagious illnesses.

Lastly, you should watch the interactions between the dogs and staff members if possible. The dogs should be vying for the attention of their caregivers.

Prices vary from one area to another, so you should also consider affordability as a factor in your decision.

The final negative to keep in mind when making a final decision about adding a Labrador to your home involves the thick coat that provides warmth and water resistance. When these functions aren't necessary, for instance, every summer, the undercoat will make an exit. This will produce a great deal of dead hair to keep under control. Some people choose to keep high shedders outside for this very reason, but remember, Labradors are social creatures and they need to be with their family indoors.

More information on shedding appears in chapter 3.

In-Home Lessons

Training is a must for all Labs, and house training is one of the first monumental hurdles for all new puppy owners.

Once you bring the pup home for the very first time, you can start teaching the new addition where you'd like them to do their business. But be patient. A pup's lack of maturity means a shorter attention span coupled, limited bladder control and a frequent need to eliminate.

The first thing to keep in mind deals with a dog's instinctual desire to keep their "cave" clean. All canines prefer to have a sleeping space devoid of excrement, so keeping a puppy in a small space allows you to take advantage of this innate drive.

Early on, you should restrict your new family member to a limited area of the house, and as the dog matures you can expand this area according to progress.

Secondly, young labs tend to eliminate in an area where they have gone before. To use this tendency to your advantage, use a specific outside area and accompany your pup there to eliminate every time. These trips need to be frequent in order to avoid indoor accidents. While the two of you are outside, you can get them accustomed to terminology that, to you, means "hurry up." A lot of people repeat the phrase, "go potty" using a gentle, low-decibel voice. Try to maintain this type of composure even when it's raining profusely or the temperature has dropped to single digits. Your puppy will most likely be in no hurry to go back inside.

In time, however, if you consistently use the verbal cues and praise the dog when he does what you wanted, he will learn too that your phrase means "hurry up."

Crate Training

Another early training opportunity involves the place where your pup will initially sleep. But first of all, it will help to understand the reasons for using a crate for your dog. All canines enjoy the security of a den, and a dog crate can satisfy this nesting-type desire. A common misunderstanding of crate use deals with an owner's lack of understanding when it comes to the theory of a den. It is not cruel to crate your pet when the item is used as a tool and not a punishment. It should not be used to excessively contain the dog, either.

When a puppy gets used to its new home, a.k.a. the crate, it will be a stand-in for a den. The attraction of the den is both shelter and security, so you will likely notice your lab going in willing. Whenever there's a need for downtime, your pup will start to stay in the crate long after you stop closing the door whenever its ready for some downtime. The crate actually provides a place your pup considers his own personal territory. It's a place that your puppy will know he can escape to whenever he's afraid or feels overwhelmed.

The benefit of incorporating a crate involves an aspect that perfectly suits the effort of house training. Remember, a dog won't eliminate in the space where it sleeps, so the crate offers the opportunity to teach control. Keep the time limited, according to age, because a puppy will soil the bedding when that is the only option.

The maximum amount of time spent crated is about six hours for a twelve-week-old Lab. This includes nighttime. When crate time is over, you should take your puppy from the crate directly to the spot that you've designated as the official the bathroom.

When your puppy has free reign in an area of your home, be sure to watch for signs that it needs to eliminate. Every dog develops its own behavior, so signals vary, but often a dog will begin sniffing around for a place to go.

The ideal time to take the puppy outside is before it begins to urinate, and the next is before it is finished. The process of house training takes patience, persistence, and consistency. More information about training is in the next chapter.

For pre-obedience training experience, you can seek out a reputable puppy class for both socialization opportunities, as well as getting you started on the right track behavior-wise. Information and tips of training appear in chapter 2.

Labs can be very vocal without corrective training.

Finding a reputable breeder

Your best bet for finding a well-balanced puppy is to look for a breeder who is associated with a reputable national association. The American Kennel Club, for instance, is one of the most widely known organizations.

Secondly, Labradors have genetic conditions that could be passed down, including serious diseases such as hip dysplasia, diabetes, and cancer.

One way to increase the odds in favor of health involves finding a puppy from certified parents. Certified means the dogs have been checked by a medical professional for all signs of inherited disease and none were found. The vet would then provide disease-free certification for the parent.

Another wise move toward finding the ideal puppy for you involves visiting with the entire litter of siblings. By observing the whole litter, you can spot any pups with divergent characteristics, such as shyness or aggression. Even one puppy with adverse behavior can be a red flag that the breeder is not up to par.

On the other hand, if all littermates have the typical friendly, exuberant, attention- seeking demeanor, odds are you'll find a well-balanced pup.

The breeder will know the exact date the puppies were born and should not be willing to send them off to new homes until they are at least six weeks old. Seven to eight weeks is preferable.

Also, a reputable breeder will readily provide health records and should have six-week vaccination already completed.

Questions to Ask a Breeder
NEEDED

Are the parents certified as disease-free?

What is the guarantee?

How large was the mother?

How large was the father?

Are both parents on the premises?

Can I meet the parents?

How much socialization have the puppies had?

What type of socialization have the puppies had?

Have there been any health issues with any of the puppies in the litter?

Sometimes the breeder will have both the mother and father on premises, allowing you to see the temperament and size potential that will pass to their offspring.

From there, you can spend time with individual pups to further see if there a love match. To check temperament, you can play with a pup one-on-one and gently turn it belly up. A moderate temperament will object a bit but will also be open to a gently wrestling match or belly rub. If a pup turns over readily, stays in that position, and looks away, it's extremely submissive and prone to problems like antisocial behavior, anxiety, and even fear aggression. The flip side would be the puppy who obstinately refuses to be belly up. This could signal a pup that will be a challenge to train.

Experienced, certified breeders caution prospective lab owners against purchasing a puppy from questionable sellers, possible puppy mills, and "backyard breeders."

When the origin of the puppy is unknown, there is a risk that the puppies will be more prone to developing breed-specific disorders, general canine health issues, and undesirable behavior due to poor breeding or inappropriate puppy rearing practices.

Longtime Labrador owner Stacy Brenner provides a strong example of the consequences endured after purchasing a puppy from a backyard breeder. This is the story she told during a recent interview.

"

Growing up, we always had Labs. They were great dogs, and I remember picking out every one of them. We went to the same breeder each time we wanted a new puppy. We had four in total.

I never really thought about where the puppies came from so when my boys wanted a dog, I bought a lab from someone local who had posted a sign about puppies for sale.

We got a girl named Clancy. She was about two months old when we brought her home, and the first year proved very challenging. The worst part initially was her urge to bite because her sharp little puppy teeth could really do some damage.

You couldn't just sit and pet her. Her first response to any attention was always to latch on to your fingers or your arm or whatever she could get her teeth around.

My children would try to pet her, and she wasn't interested in anything but sinking her teeth in.

She didn't do it viciously, of course. She had that typically fun-loving Lab personality. She was just taught that it was okay.

She didn't come from a breeder that had credentials or any AKC-type memberships, so I think the puppies in the litter got a lot of experience playing roughly. When we were picking out Clancy, I did notice the kids who lived there like to get the puppies riled up to where they would grab onto their arms and bite. The kids laughed when they did. I guess it's cute when puppies don't have sharp teeth yet.

But Clancy had been allowed to play bite, and it was hard to break her off that behavior. As she got older and her teeth became sharper, it was a real problem.

She would pull on everyone's pants legs and put a lot of holes in our clothes that way. My youngest son, when Clancy got bigger, she could reach the hem of his shirt. He was scared of her for a while because she would tug on his shirt so hard that she would make him fall.

We got advice about what to do from an obedience trainer, but it took a lot of time and patience.

The method that the trainer had us do was, every time she would start to bite, we had to stop playing immediately and turn our backs toward her. Ignoring the behavior was hard when she'd start pulling on your clothes, but there really was nothing else to do.

It took time and a lot of hole in our clothes, but she learned. She didn't like not getting attention. Even so, I think she was almost a year old before the behavior subsided completely.

I could really tell the difference between Clancy's behavior and the dogs we had growing up. Clancy mentally remained a puppy for close to three years. She was always a good dog, and Labs do tend to have a puppy mentality for longer than most breeds, but it took her a very long time to grow up.

We had a few good years, but she never really calmed down, not until she started getting sick. First, we noticed tumors along her spine when she was about six years old. She also developed diabetes, then bursitis, and finally, we found out one of the tumors on her spine was cancerous.

There really was nothing they could do for her. Toward the end, she really had no quality of life. She needed help getting up. We had to use a hammock-type device under her backside to help her walk. It was hard to see, but even harder to make the call to have her put to sleep.

Despite all she'd been through, she still had such a sweet personality. I know she loved every one of us. And it's such a shame that this happened because someone thought it would be fun to see their dog have puppies. Well, it wasn't fun for us. And it certainly wasn't fun for Clancy.

It was heartbreaking. I learned my lesson, though. I'll never get a puppy from a situation like that again. Not ever.

"

Be Prepared for Homecoming

After you find a good breeder and choose your new puppy, keep in mind that everything about the initial introduction to a new home will have a lasting effect. Try to keep the experience positive and free of stressors for the new member of the family. You will want to introduce your puppy to members of the family gradually if there are many children in the household. Be sure to instruct the children to remain calm and only use slow, gentle motions when approaching the puppy for the first time.

The puppy has just been taken from his own brothers and sisters and from the only home its known for the first part of life. As you can imagine, this experience could cause a great deal of anxiety and uncertainty about what is taking place. Any excitement, even when it's positive, can prove overwhelming for your puppy when so many changes are happening at once. Keep this mind and be sure everyone understands this idea before having contact with the puppy. At first, you might want to keep the puppy in one small room while the initial adjustment is taking place. This will help the puppy feel more secure and less intimidated by excessive space.

Also, keep in mind that the excitement could

prompt urination, so keep an eye out for any signs that your puppy is ready to go outside. It's never too soon to work on positive training. And all accidents hinder the process, even those that result from excitement.

New Territory

Everything should be set up and all supplies on hand before you bring the puppy through the door. Part of the task of preparedness involves ensuring the area designated for the puppy is free from breakables, choking hazards, and all of products containing chemicals of any kind. Think of how you would childproof an area for a two-year-old human and apply the same measures for your puppy's space.

Also, it's a good idea for someone in the household to be available for a few consecutive days to spend time with the pup to help ease the transition. Remember, the dog has spent every moment since birth surround by littermates, the mother, and attending breeders. The sudden move to isolation in unfamiliar territory could have negative and lasting consequence. For instance, it readily sets the stage for potential bouts of destructive behavior and even separation anxiety down the line. Labs are friendly, social creatures, and your presence in the first days will prompt bonding to begin. This social tendency is also the reason having someone on hand during the first few days will help the puppy feel more comfortable. It's also a good idea to have some Lab-friendly toys in the puppy's area. If anxiety or nervousness seem excessive a game of fetch could be the key to directing the mood in a more positive direction. Again, be aware of timing where potty training is concerned. If your puppy has had a big serving of water, you can plan to take a trip outside about 10 minutes later. All dogs are different, though, and the timing could be earlier or later than the average. Monitor your puppy's particular internal clock and plan bathroom breaks accordingly.

Also look for signs your puppy needs to go. Many dogs will begin sniffing around, but for a hunting breed, they may do nothing but sniff around. Keep a watch for your puppy's particular signs. Once you have an idea about signs and a schedule be sure to provide this information to everyone in the household. As you will learn in upcoming chapters, consistency and routine are key behavior development. Inconsistency and mixed signals could bring on behavior that isn't so desirable.

What's for Dinner?

Food is obviously a necessity, but quality nutrition and puppy-specific types are the best way to go.

First of all, Labradors grow from a couple of pounds and top at eighty pounds in the course of a year. That's an enormous increase, equaling nearly seventy-five times the birth weight in only twelve months. While your pup is growing, a lot of changes are happening quickly as well. That's of a lot of change during the course of twelve months, so you'll need food specifically designed for larger breeds. Upper brands can provide the correct balance a lab needs to support joints, bones, cranial development, and appropriate weight.

Nutrition in puppyhood provides the baseline for your dog's overall health in the long run. More information on brand options and feeding guidelines appears in chapter 3. For now, keep in mind that Lab puppies will eat no matter how full their stomachs get. Don't count on signals from your puppy about whether they are hungry or full. You will need to pay attention to the serving suggestions provided on the label of the food as a guideline for portions. You should also not leave a bowl of food out without limits on how much your puppy eats daily. Obesity is a concern in all stages of life, and starting off with too much weight during puppyhood can lead to continued, lifelong issues.

Basic Training—It's a Must

T he first rule to follow starts the moment you bring your puppy home. Reward your pup for all the good behavior and, when possible, ignore the bad.

Labs of all ages thrive on attention, and the lack

of attention will go a long way for this breed. Every time your puppy does something you would rather not see continue, don't explain your reasoning or tell the pup "no, don't do that." Even when you are obviously upset, your speech and eye contact are considered attention.

When safety allows, you can turn your back toward the puppy, and this signal will be much more effective in curbing unwanted behavior. This same technique will work in most situations, with the exception of potty training and chewing inedible objects. The latter behavior is most likely one you will see before the end of puppyhood. Labs have a big urge to use their mouths. This is a result of their intent. The breed was first used to retrieve, of course, and to do so required a dog with a strong like for mouthing. Modern situations rarely offer a plethora of opportunity to soothe this instinctual desire, so Labs will want to find satisfaction through alternatives. These alternatives take the form of slippers, wood, articles of clothing, or plastic bottles. This is the reason why elimination all hazardous chemicals and safety hazards from the are your puppy is allowed to roam. This include outside areas where there could be boards with nails, trash items such bottles both glass and plastic and anything else your puppy might take an interest in

Instead, be sure to include options that are more appropriate for your puppy to consume. There are a wide variety of chew toys that satisfy the chewing urge without adding calories. One choice of entertainment is an item made by Kong that will provide a rubbery chew sensation, with the perk of having a hollow cone shape that allows space for treats. Your puppy will remain entertained for a while as it works to get the food from the inside of the Kong. Be sure to get the correct size. Some Kongs are made for small dogs and are not strong enough to stand up to the teeth of a Lab pup.

Read labels closely and be sure to get the correct size and durability to suit a young Lab.

These chew toys can remain a tool for entertaining your dog throughout all stages of life. Be warned, though, that Kongs can be a tool for your dog also. It's not uncommon for them to come to your repeatedly, with Kong in mouth, asking for refills. You'll know their coming for treats when, from behind, you hear a breathy, Darth Vader-like sound getting closer and closer. The noise is your dog's breath rushing through the hole of empty Kong.

Active Intervention

When the negative acts, like chew inappropriate items, requires interaction, use body language that expresses your dislike for the behavior. You can clean up, take away, or do what the crime necessitates, but do so without speaking. Maintain an expression of disapproval, and when you've intervened sufficiently to amend the situation, turn your back to the puppy and withhold attention for the moment. These two approaches will help steer your pup away from negative actions before repetition solidifies the unwanted behavior. The intervention is necessary for safety reasons, but can be kept to a minimum so attention will not become a reward for the action.

Puppies Will Be Puppies

Don't forgo puppy class because your puppy hasn't reached the point where training produces obvious benefits. Activity among peers provides the opportunity for your pup to learn social manners before they mature to a point where negative behavior, due to a lack of direction and appropriate social interaction, becomes permanent or at least difficult to cure.

Yes, puppies haven't reached the level of maturity required for serious obedience training, but that's not the point of this prerequisite course. It's an introduction to a structured environment where your pup can socialize and learn some manners or, at the very least, friendly interaction before adult instincts kick in. Due to short attention spans during puppyhood, don't expect too much from your pet too soon. Keep the practice fun and pressure-free.

Basic Puppy Training

Training can be a great bonding experience for you and your puppy, both in a structured class and during practice sessions at home. The stronger the connection you have with your puppy, the stronger the urge you puppy will have to show behavior that you want to see.

Bonding comes as a result of the time you spend with your dog. From calm petting sessions and gentle grooming to games of Frisbee and dashing through puddles.

These shared activities will help your puppy build trust and confidence in your leadership and alliance. The togetherness will also strengthen camaraderie for both you and dog, and often these bonds will drive dogs to great lengths. Stories abound about what dogs will endure out of love. There's the story of a dog whose family members moved across the country without taking him along. The dog miraculously showed up at the door of the family's new home months after the move. He was skinny with a visible rib cage. His coat was matted and muddy. And his tongue was out with his tail wagging when his family members opened the door. The dog had tracked his family for hundreds of miles with hopes for a reunion.

Additionally, there are heartbreaking stories of dogs whose love remained strong years after their masters had passed. One dog remained at the gravesite of the man who had raised him from puppyhood, never going more than ten or fifteen feet from the headstone. The dog lived years longer than the man, but he refused all offers for a new home. Whenever a family would try to take him in, before long the dog would find his way back to grave site. His loyalty never died. He slept with his side against the marker night after night, surviving on water and table scraps people would bring for him, until finally he passed, on that same plot of land.

This human-canine connection is instinctual for both parties. For dogs, it comes from their innate desire to be a pack member and to be included. Then, of course, you hear stories of dogs who died protecting their handlers, or who leapt between their owner and a bolt of lightning, giving their lives to save theirs.

This bond is ancient. And through the right kind and frequency of shared experiences, the strength becomes unbreakable. Without sufficient interaction, however, the connection weakens, and the relationship fails to form.

You can monitor the strength of the bond you have with your puppy through signals that will be obvious.

You can feel love for your dog without having those feelings reciprocated when shared activity is insufficient. Some signals of that situation include an attitude of indifference. Your dog will interact at times, but it's not an activity that he initiates. He will most likely lose interest quickly and move on to doing solo activities.

A weak bond could be the cause of your dog's unwillingness to obey commands, especially the recall command. Why would a dog readily return to an owner that they don't feel close to? An unattached dog might show signs of aggression or even have bouts of depression. Dogs innately want to be a member of a social group and without realization of this desire; their basics needs go unfulfilled.

If your dog routinely bolts out the door at every opportunity or doesn't seem interested in your affection, odds are some bonding work is in order.

Signs your bond is weak

- Indifference to you and other family members
- No desire for interaction
- Avoidance of contact

- Repeated attempts to run away from home
- No eye contact
- Undesirable behavior
- Disobedience
- Low spirits

Start your partnership off right by letting your pup know what you expect and providing praise for good behavior. Training is a process that takes patience, positivity, and small steps.

As with all other activities, strive for keeping things upbeat and minimize any pressure for the puppy to excel at a faster pace than maturity levels can handle. You should also gauge your own stress level because patience is essential to the success of the training.

Basic commands and obedience should be taught from the stance of positive reinforcement. Never punish your pup for falling short of expectations. This includes speaking in a harsh tone or using your voice at higher than speaking decibels.

Negative feedback will only lessen your pet's confidence, trust, and sense of security, impeding the progress of training.

Most trainers who offer puppy basic classes will demonstrate positive reinforcement methods used to keep the experience stress-free and on course. This positive reinforcement includes treats and praise delivered in response to something your pup performs correctly.

Not all trainers condone treats as a reinforcer due to the added calories that may affect the balance of the pet's nutritional needs.

Because Labs are readily aiming to please their owners, praise from the handler is sometimes all the reward the breed requires to keep up the good work.

Additionally, with the issue of overeating and obesity common with Labs, it's best to not overdo the delivery of treats.

Eventually, treats won't be necessary once your pup responds appropriately to a command in succession. Just a smile or slight acknowledgment of good work will suffice.

Of course, house training will already be a work in progress from the day, but that undertaking can happen simultaneously with the introduction of basic commands.

A typical puppy class serves as a springboard for future obedience training and includes socialization opportunities as well as a lesson on simple commands.

Class requirements vary, so find out what tools

will be required before the day of the class. Basics you should already have on hand include a proper-fitting collar and a standard leash. Those items are all most trainers will require throughout the class.

Who Should Attend/Be the Handler

There should be one or two family members who consistently attend every class. It's best if one person becomes the appointed trainer of the family. The same person works with the puppy in class as well as practice times. When a trick or command response reaches a consistent level of success, other family members can become involved. This will help alleviate confusion when one person deviates from the method used by another. Remember consistency and repetition produce behaviors that become habitual. That can work for both negative and positive input.

At some point during puppy school, the instructor could demonstrate effective methods for getting puppies accustomed to leashes (frequently referred to at leads), but the main focus remains on supervised play and interaction practice. Typically, you will have time to ask questions in a block of time either at the beginning or before the end of class.

You should ask about any behavioral concerns you have during specified times so you can get the most out of practice time with your puppy. It's not uncommon for new pet owners to have a lot of questions. When the time to ask arrives, however, it's also common to not remember everything you meant to ask about.

As you reach the last classes of puppy school, you would typically begin setting the stage for upcoming basic command training. Typically, this is the next class level you would need.

Some organization, though, offer more than one level of puppy class. The initial level provides a controlled environment where puppies learn to interact with other dogs and also unfamiliar people. This positive exposure happens under the supervision and direction of a professional who can observe behavior, looking for any red flags that might become problematic with correction. The basics, such as lead walking and teaching the first commands, could be introduced during the course of the introductory class, but the next level provides the first real training practice. Both puppy classes, however, are more about interaction than obedience.

In a puppy II level class, experienced pups will again have the opportunity for social interaction, but more lead work and more practice with commands will most likely take place.

When puppies take their first walk around the

circle, there is usually more time spent chewing on leashes than walking. At this level, introduction is mainly the extent of the lesson.

To work on the sit command, the instructor might have you voice the command and introduce a hand motion at the same time. This will teach the dog to sit when the command is issued only by motion. Hand signals are good to use as a backup in the event you need to make an order where there is a lot of noise or when silence is essential.

To begin the first practice of sit, instructors using positive reinforcement will ask you to hold a small piece of treat between your thumb and first finger. You will tell your dog to sit as you show the treat, then you slowly raise your hand from in front of the nose toward the top of the head.

As puppies watch the treat go up, they tend to

automatically drop into a sitting position. When they do, they get a treat. If they don't then the first part is repeated. Once the puppy catches on, you would still do the hand motion, but instead of a treat, provide attention and verbal praise.

You can continue practicing at home but remember to limit the work to five-minute sessions and end on a positive note.

Between puppy classes, you should also work on social skills. Appropriate interaction with both people and other pets during the first months of puppies' lives plays a major role in helping them become well-adjusted adults.

During this window of opportunity in puppyhood, try to expose your pup to a variety of people, places, and animals.

Getting young dogs used to children during

puppyhood will curb the tendency most canines have to go into high alert around anyone less than three feet tall. Many dogs have an instinctual aversion to small children and when this instinct isn't dispelled, the uncertainty can sometimes times lead to fear-driven acts of aggression.

To help get dogs used to children, you would want to initially introduce them to one or two children who you are certain will remain calm and gentle.

Again, when spending time in various situations, remember to reward the behavior you want to see your dog continue. The positive reinforcement helps relay the message about how you expect them to act during encounters with non-family members.

Of course, you'll still need to intervene if your

pup's behavior poses any type of safety risk, especially in the company of children.

In a nutshell, training your Lab at any stage of obedience has the same basic formula—reward the good and ignore the bad.

Make a List of Worrisome Behaviors

All dogs will develop their own good and bad traits, and it's best to address any concerns as early as possible. Puppy and future obedience classes provide a source of support and advice to help you curb negative behavior as soon as you see a trend.

You can make a list of behaviors that you would like to correct as close as possible to the time they happen. It's too easy to forget what you *meant* to write down earlier and even easier to forget once you get to class sans list. The week between classes, as the behavior continues, more time is lost in finding cures. One way to keep up with topics of concern is to keep a notebook in a convenient place all the time.

When something happens that you want to ask about, you can write it down before it slips your mind. When it's close to class time, take a picture of the lists using your cellphone and you'll most likely have your questions with you when it's time for Q and A.

Your list of issues could contain a wide range of unwelcome conduct, from simple slipper chewing to displaying aggressive behavior, either toward people, other pets or in specific situations.

Whether the behavior poses a big problem or it's an activity that you prefer your pup not continue, the longer you wait to take appropriate corrective measures, the more permanent the behavior becomes. Puppy class is the place to discuss worrisome tendency with a professional trainer.

Once you receive advice and start working to correct bad tendencies, you need to make sure that all family members follow suit.

For example, your pup begs for food every time someone has a snack or the family sits down for dinner, the behavior will continue if any one person gives in. Even randomly passing along table scraps can ruin every effort you have already put forth. So, don't let those sad brown eyes thwart your progress. And the same goes for everyone either living in or visiting your home.

The habit of sharing people food with your dog poses, not only bothersome antics, but the additional calories could pave the way for weight gain and even obesity.

Big Bad Behavior

It's not always easy to identify aggressive behavior during the puppy stages, but the signs will be evident when you know how they look.

A young pup who acts fearless, especially around other animals or children, could be en route to becoming an aggressive adult dog. Being alert to the signs will give you a preemptive chance to change the direction.

Aside from signs of extreme bravery, be wary of times when your puppy seems to be standing tall and hyper-alert. This could be an attempt to appear more sizable, and thus more intimidating. A show of **aggression** can include a puffed-out chest, a long and straight tail position, and hair standing on end along the nape of the neck and past the shoulders.

Obviously growling shows aggressive intent, but one not so obvious is a wagging tail. The swish of the tail might bring relief when you think it means your pup is simply being playful. But if the wag is moving slowly back and forth, think of it as the way a cat swishes its tail when its sights are set on prey.

Submissiveness is not so opposite a problem.

An overly submissive or shy dog can be just as worrisome as one with aggression issues. Fear presents as much potential for growling, snipping and even biting.

Signs from a submissive dog are mostly the direct opposite of those from one with an aggressive nature. Instead of trying to look larger, an overly shy dog will cower down to minimize its size. You could also notice submissive signs that include the tail positioned low and often tucked down between the back legs. The tail may also be wagging, but again, not because the dog is feeling playful. The wagging communicates non-threatening intent. A show of affection or rolling over with the belly up are attempts to communicate that same message.

Both aggression and submission represent negative behavior that trainers can help you work to correct.

Hear Me Out

Part of a dog's method of communication involves noises that range from simply annoying to extremely problematic. Whining, for example, is your pup's way of expressing a need, and typically either food or attention is the object of desire.

The whimpering proves a bit nerve-racking when

it's constant, and trainers can give you some tips for curbing the undesirable vocalizing. But rarely do the low-decibel whines prompt complaints from outside the homestead.

Excessive barking, on the other hand, could initiate a feud with anyone living within earshot, and even worse, depending on ordinances for your area, the noise could bring substantial fines. Even if there are no local laws that directly address the issue of barking, your dog's vocalizing could violate a general noise ordinance, which most towns have in place.

Violations in various areas of the United States have come with steep consequences, from thousands of dollars in fines to ten-day jail sentences.

If you begin working early with an overly vocal pup, you will hopefully never need to contend with such issues. One thing about barking to keep in mind, though, is that it's an instinctual and natural mode of communication for dogs. Dogs need to bark. It's only when the response becomes excessive that corrective measures are in order.

No matter the noise, whether it's whimpers, howls, yaps, or barks, if the level of occurrence causes concern, speak to the obedience class instructor. The teacher can help you assess the level and suggest ways to correct anything past the norm.

On your own, however, the strategy to consistently use is simple: Ignore the bad and reward the good.

If you scold or give comfort while your dog is whining, you're delivering attention and this "reward" encourages the unwanted behavior. It is when the whining stops that you respond with something positive, such as praise or playful interaction. This reaction will teach your pup the type of behavior you expect from them.

The same technique holds true for barking. Telling a dog to be quiet while they are in a fit of barking is not only a fruitless undertaking, it's also counterproductive to what you are hoping to achieve. Again, any interaction is attention, so telling your dog to stop barking will most likely beget more barking. Wait until the dog is quiet, and then reward the silence.

The withholding of attention is not a cure-all, but it's a place to start when you first notice inappropriate behavior.

Time to Work

Next, pick only one trick at a time. (This does not

include house training, remember.) Puppies aren't ready to multi-task, so choose one command to work on, and practice only the one, for a maximum of five minutes at a time. When that command becomes automatic or at least until fails are minimal, move on to the next command, and again stick to practicing just that one. Always keep sessions short, but you can also throw in a single practice here and there whenever the opportunity arises.

Keep It Consistent

Perfecting any skill takes practice. A puppy learns by performing the same exercise over and over. But keep in mind that the learning process also requires a format for the practice that never deviates from one session to the next.

If you expect the same response when you issue a command, you need to deliver the order in a set format every single time. Otherwise, your dog won't know that various approaches all involve just one command.

Consistency and practice make perfect when it comes to training your puppy. Use only one word per command. If you are teaching your dog not to jump up on the couch, be sure to say "off" and use the same motion every time. Your dog won't understand that "off" and "down" mean the same thing to you. Pick one and stick with it. Visual cues help also, but only if you do the same motion every time. If you point to the floor one time initially but make several pointing gestures the next, this will look like two separate directions to your dog. Keep it simple and consistent and make sure everyone in the household uses the exact same delivery.

Mix It Up

Now that you've mastered consistency, it's time to mix things up, but only scenery-wise. Your pup will need to understand that you want him to obey the command regardless of location. It may be easier to begin a new command and practice in the same designated area at first. But once your pup is catching on, be sure to test out the command in various spots inside and out, and add in a mix of distractions when the command response becomes automatic. Test this mastery against the smell of food cooking, or near a busy ballfield. By mixing up the practice field, your pup will know to obey the command every time and in every place you give the order.

Also, your dog needs to understand that it is required to obey a command issued from anyone in the household, not just you. Having other family members practice command response can teach your pup the order of the pack, the pecking order so to speak.

Recall Command in Puppyhood

Even before the first class begins, you can begin teaching puppies when they are eight weeks old and up. The best basic command to work on first is teaching your pup to come when you call. For this practice, you can hold your own training sessions at home. Plan to limit the amount of time you spend on each training session, keeping 10 minutes the absolute maximum. The level of maturity dictates the length of a dog's attention span, and for a puppy, both aspects are in short supply.

Pushing past reasonable expectations will test your patience and impede progress. Even when a session hasn't been the best experience, find a way to conclude the training with a positive feel.

Every puppy has its own likes and dislikes, so find a reward that is meaning for your unique pet. A favorite toy, treat or activity can move you both in a more positive direction

The recall or "come" command is the most life-saving behavior your puppy will learn, so it's best to begin building the base as early as possible. If your puppy gets in a precarious situation but has a solid grasp on the recall command, it could prevent your pup from entering a busy road.

Day One

To begin the training, it's best to find an area with ample room and limited distractions. On day one, the lesson could be as simple as introducing the word. When both of you are calm, you can say the word "come" and follow up with an act of praise or a small treat, like a piece of kibble. This will present a positive experience that the puppy will associate with the command. That will serve as the entirety of the lesson.

Each day you can build on, according to the progress of the previous day. For example, on day two, you can return to the same area, but this time, instead of handing the treat directly to your pup, drop it somewhere close to both of you.

After the pup has found and eaten the treat, wait until you make eye contact, then say the command. For the second day, you can keep the activity simple and repeat the same action two or three more times before calling it a day.

Day Two and Beyond

From there, increase the challenge according to your dog's achievement, making sure to not move too fast for your pup's level of success.

To do this, try dropping the treat at varying distances away and work up to a point where you can toss it further with the same reaction. After the treat is finished off, make sure your puppy looks toward you again before saying the word "come." You can also begin adding the dog's name when you say the command so it will learn to return to you when you say either or both words.

To keep the training moving, extend the distance you toss the treat. Be sure not to push past the point of success. If your dog fails to look toward you after finishing the treat, go back to the last point of success and work from there again.

When you're ready to move on, you can toss the treat as before, but when your dog makes eye contact, say the command as you take a couple steps in the opposite direction. This becomes a game of chase as you progress so will provide some exercise for you both as well.

Change It Up

The next step forward involves practicing this activity in other places, both inside and outside if possible. Always be sure to do this work inside a fenced in area or in a space that will keep the puppy confined in a safe place.

When these options aren't available, most pet stores carry long leashes, sometimes with lengths reaching two hundred feet, that are made specifically for training purposes. These provide a suitable alternative to open space training.

Regardless of the location or whether you're practicing on or off leash, be sure to keep this a fun and positive experience. You should always praise your pup generously every time it comes to you, even when you are not specifically practicing this command.

Keep It Positive

Make this positive reinforcement a habit so your dog knows to expect good things every time it returns to you. On the flip side, you never want to call your dog to you for the purpose of scolding or punishment. For example, your precious puppy has decided to test out new chew toy options, and you discover this only after a good portion of your new glasses remains toothmark free. This is not the time to practice the recall command.

Similarly, you wouldn't want to call your puppy to come to you when it's bath time. Not many dogs look forward to grooming, so you would need to bring the puppy to the tub. If you call your pup to you for bath time, don't expect the next recall practice to go without a hitch. The puppy now associates a less than pleasant experience with responding to the command.

Be sure to call your puppy to you only for positive reasons. Pet them. Praise them. Provide a reason for them to always want to come when you call. You don't want your puppy to ever hesitate in a life-or-death situation. The response needs to remain immediate.

You can work more on this command in a structured obedience training class. Initially, though, your puppy needs to learn some manners. Those lessons will be part of the reason you'll want to sign up for puppy classes. These structured play times lay the groundwork for future obedience development and formation of a socially well-adjusted companion. The biggest benefit your pup gains from school is learning appropriate social behavior.

At home, in class, or with a training doing one-on-one practice, be sure your dog has ample opportunity to learn to behave. It's a good choice for both of you.

Before choosing a class or type of training, check credentials and contact reference if possible. The most reliable information comes from previous customers, so ask for suggestions. You can also find information from past customers by searching online. For example, you can enter "dog trainers near me" and a list of local options will come up in a list that includes Google ratings for each one. These ratings offer customers a chance to use the five-star system to represent their experience level. This means training courses that receive only one star would be the least likely choice if many people gave this low of a rating. Conversely, the classes with many five-star ratings would be the place you would want to start investigating. Typically, people are able to include comments explaining the number of stars chosen, and this information is helpful to learn about the particular services that prompted unfavorable responses.

Of course, with the search returns, there will be contact information and, if applicable, a link to the website of the training provider. You shouldn't rely solely on the ratings to make your final decision. You will benefit from directly discussing training philosophies with the instructor prior to committing to an entire series of classes. There is a wide range of approaches to obedience, and you want to make sure the instructor has an approach that you feel comfortable putting into practice.

One example of varied philosophies deals with the issue of play biting. Some trainers, as the one mentioned previously, opt for avoidance when dealing with negative behavior. With this approach, you would withhold attention when any unwanted behavior surfaces, including play biting. When the behavior isn't taking place or when it stops, you would then give some form of positive reinforcement, such as a piece of kibble or verbal praise.

On the other hand, there is a school of thought that direct contact immediately draws attention to the negative consequences that happen when biting takes place. The direct contact some instructors teach involves tapping the dog with the flat of your open hand under its chin.

The tapping increases if the dog continually fails to stop the behavior. The problem most owners have with this method involves trust issues. It's important for a dog to have complete trust in their owner to keep the pet's focus on wanting to please the owner. Instilling fear isn't compatible with building trust.

The vet you choose can also be a good source for recommendations.

Agility Training

Labradors aim to please—generally speaking. This quality, along with their sporting features, makes the breed good candidates for agility training.

Basically, the trainer can be added at the end of standard obedience training classes. These activities start simply by teaching your dog how to weave their way through a line of traffic cones. Initially, you will use small bits of treats that you dangle in front of the nose to lead them in and out appropriately.

As you go, you randomly deliver tidbits of treats from beginning to end. A word of caution here for owners who have dogs with a hyper-focus on food. This exercise could result in accidentally bite marks on your fingers when your dog eagerly accepts the treats. One way to avoid this issue involves using one hand to direct and using hour free hand to hold the treats. Every so often, you will put a tidbit on the flat of the leading hand. This can be tricky, and your dog might follow the hand with the food. If this method proves unsuccessful, you can experiment with various gloves and tape wrapping for protection. The good news is you will eventually do away with the treats when your dog learns the trick.

Another part of beginning agility often proves difficult for most of the class. The challenge has nothing to do with ability or the level of difficulty with execution. It has to do with overcoming fear. Many dogs and all creatures hesitate to go into a dark tunnel when there is no visible light at the end.

This scenario is exactly what the canines face when introduced to the Chute. The chute is merely a flexible wire tunnel covered with fabric that extends past several feet past the end of the tunnel. The problem for dogs is they often don't see the chute in entirety. They typically are introduced to the mouth of the tunnel and prompted to run through, even though they see no opening in the other end.

It takes many tries for some dogs to muster enough courage. When the dogs make it through the chute one time, though, it is difficult to get them not to run through from then on.

There occasionally will be a dog that never finds the end of the chute. When anxiety gets high near the middle of the tunnel, sometimes the student turns back and exits where it entered.

Other exercises practiced at various stages of agility include the catwalk, which is similar to walking a tightrope except the dogs walk along a narrow board at heights that vary depending on the level of the class.

Other activities teach dogs to slide down slides and jump through tire swings. The experience is a fun way to bond while your dog learns new skills and burns a lot of energy. For those Labs that excel in agility class, competitions are a possibility. Most likely, instructor of obedience classes can recommend agility trainers in your area.

Nutrition and Healthcare

P roviding your puppy with the balance of nutrition required for proper growth will set a solid of quality kibble, breed-specific formulations, and types with ingredients to suit special needs and breed-specific.

Once you find the right one for your puppy, there's no need for supplements or the addition of anything from the kitchen. Fill their bowl with the recommended portion for the meal, according to instructions from your vet and the manufacturer's recommendations. Also, make sure your pup has fresh water throughout the day. If you have a sizable space where your puppy is allowed to spend time, you should consider having a second dish of water place in another location in the area. Your puppy, then, is sure to get enough water to help ensure urinary tract health.

Food shouldn't be readily supplied, however. The proper amount of each daily ration gets divided into meals that you serve at different times of the day. For instance, you would fill the dish with one-third of the food in the morning, one-third in the afternoon, and the rest in the evening.

Keeping the bowl filled with food without

attention to the amount is not recommended, especially with the tendency Labs have to overconsume.

Breed-Specific Options

When you begin your search for the puppy food, where you go to—the grocery or a pet store—you'll find an overwhelming number of choices. So where do you start?

First, look for a brand that offers formulas made to suit the nutritional needs of large breed dogs. Some brands offer Labrador-specific formulas instead of a general mix for multiple breeds. Either way, make sure you get a puppy formula geared toward the size your pup will be as an adult.

Canines are carnivores, so the next thing to do is read labels. If meat is not at the top on the list of ingredients, reshelve the bag and move on. When you find one that meets this requirement, pay attention to the way the meat is defined. Does only the name of the meat appear on the label, or is it followed by some defining term, such as meal or by-product?

There is a difference. When you see "chicken" on the label, you know the food contains simply the meat of the animal. On the other hand, meat labeled as "chicken meal" or "chicken byproduct" means the ingredients used could contain any combination parts ground together. Often those parts include carcasses with meat remnants, skin, bones, and undeveloped eggs.

There are varying opinions about the quality of nutrition provided by the addition of the non-meat animal parts, but keep in mind nutritional facts are easier to pinpoint when using meat alone. Calcium plays a big role in proper development of larger breed puppies, and too much or too little can negatively affect developing joints.

Many dog food manufacturers have joined the grain-free, gluten-free movement to provide the same nutrients without ingredients that could potentially lead to inflammation and digestive issues. This is a big plus because the addition of those ingredients isn't necessary. Neither grain nor gluten is a staple in the carnivore diet. Those items have been traditionally added more for bulk more than actual nutritional value.

For the right balance of nutrition, look for the highest quality brand you can afford. Price doesn't always mean a better product so don't go with food based solely on cost.

Market versus Premium

You can find food packages touting "premium," "ultra-premium," and other buzzwords used for marketing purposes. There is no question that there is a disparate level of quality in the range of pet foods on shelves in both grocery stores and specialty pet stores. The number of choices alone can be daunting when trying to choose what best fits both your budget and the nutritional needs of your puppy.

Premium brands often provide a precise balance of nutrients and, of course, will cost more than brands found in grocery stores. It's never too early to ward off common large breed health issues, one being joint inflammation and the development of hip dysplasia. Puppy food with the appropriate balance of calcium can help improve your pup's odds against developing such disorders.

When in doubt, consult your veterinary for advice on providing the correct balance of nutrition your puppy will need to become a well-developed adult companion.

Food Quality

The varying quality of ingredients from one brand of food to another has many facets to consider when budgeting for nutritional needs. Premium foods come at a premium price, but they typically offer more whole food ingredients, fewer fillers, and fewer preservatives.

While the dollar-per-pound is higher, the premium brands typically offer higher concentrations of nutrients so smaller portions can meet the ideal nutritional needs. More inexpensive brands add fillers such as corn, wheat, and soy, which means your puppy will need larger amounts to get the necessary nutrients.

Fillers rarely offer much nutritional value and will inevitably pass through your puppy's system, meaning more potty breaks for your pup and more cleanup work for you. The one rule to remember when it comes to nutrition is to buy the best you can afford.

High versus Low

Wellness CORE Grain Free Large Breed Puppy Food has made the top of many dog experts list of recommendations.

The manufacturer describes the protein-rich formula as a design based on the ancestral nutritional needs of canines. The label contains only a handful of ingredients. and none of them are the typical fillers, like wheat or soy, found in inexpensive varieties of puppy food. The high-quality whole meat and nutrient-dense superfoods that are in the recipe also make it one of the more expensive brands on the market. The price varies from one seller to another, but the average is $36 for a twelve-pound bag.

Another brand that makes the list of recommendations is "Taste of the Wild High Prairie Puppy Formula Grain-Free Dry Dog Food," which runs an average of $31 for a fifteen-pound bag

The formula is also based on the science of ancestral nutritional needs, and while it is a more expensive brand, the current price is a notch below CORE.

Another brand that is often touted by experts is "Blue Buffalo Wilderness High Protein Grain Free Natural Puppy Dry Dog." Again this is a high- end product with a price averaging $29 for a fifteen-pound bag.

Hill's Science Diet brand has a long history as a premium brand and breed-specific puppy food is one of the products the manufacturer offers. Their price is along the lines of the previously mentioned top brands, but if your puppy takes a liking to this one in particular, you will have many options available to choose from in all stages of your dog's life.

Mid-Range Food

IAMS is a more affordable, mid-range brand, and the manufacturer offers a variety of formulas. The puppy food geared toward larger breeds is called "Smart Puppies" and the manufacturer states the addition of Omega-3 DHA supports brain development. One of the stand-out features of the adult dog food involves products geared specifically to Labrador retrievers and not just a general large-breed formula.

The downside is found on the ingredient list, which is quite extensive and includes grain, corn, and various tocopherols. The products have been sold in pet stores for decades, but more recently, the familiar green bags appeared on grocery store shelves. This feature of location provides the perk of convenience in addition to a lower price tag when compared to higher-end brands.

A fifteen-pound bag averages from $16 to $18.

Pedigree has come into the spotlight as a recommended affordable option and the recent release of grain-free formulas. The brand offers a wide variety of recipes targeted for various stages of life. Pedigree does offer breed size-specific formula and special diet options. Most products contain ingredients like corn, wheat, and preservatives, but one plus is the omission sugar and artificial flavors. A fifteen-pound bag averages $10 to $12.

There are many, many more brands, each with multiple product lines that have a choice of ingredients. Pet stores often have several aisles designated for dog food and the options can be overwhelming. Remember look for one with a short ingredient list that is devoid of food dyes, fillers, and preservatives. And if you have a pup with a picky palate who turns down the good stuff, you may have to try a number of recipes before finding a match. Alternatively, consult your veterinary for advice on food options specifically suitable for your one-of-a-kind pup.

Treats

Treats, chews, and all those extra between-meal-type goodies that go with training and satisfying food urges. These items must also be the best affordable quality to ensure the health of your new pup.

When training, one practice that will help limit the guesswork involves keeping a handful of kibble aside from the daily portion of regular dog food to use as positive reinforcement while training. Some dogs find this offering less reinforcing than others. If your pup doesn't consider kibble much of a treat, you can invest in quality treats. The same rules for choosing good food also apply to buying treats. Many premium dog foods also offer their own line of treats. This is helpful if you have already found the right food for your puppy. Go with the same brand of treats when possible to ensure better compatibility between the two products.

Remember to consider the added calories from the treats and adjust meal portions accordingly.

When you need to search for treats beyond your brand of pet food, look for quality ingredients. Remember to look for one with the fewest amount of ingredients on the label.

Also, avoid excessive amounts of grain, corn and other ingredients that could cause digestive issues. Labs are notoriously over-indulgent and will usually accept all food that comes their way. When adding treats to their diet, try to keep the amount given to a minimum. And remember to keep treats and bags of food out of reach.

When calories and food portions aren't patrolled, the resulting excess weight is not the biggest concern for overeaters. Too many calories on a daily basis can cause a pup to grow too fast. This expedited growth can negatively affect bone quality and proper skeletal formation.

Labradors, being a larger breed, are particularly predisposed to serious consequences that occur from growing too quickly.

Often, books and online content about puppy care present generic schedules of feeding, but no one schedule fits all puppies and all brands of food. To get a general idea about proper amounts to feed according to age and weight, your vet is a better source of advice. Also, keep in mind that foods differ from one brand to the next. Some higher quality foods are nutrient-rich and require smaller amounts per serving. You would be better off using the product specific guidelines listed on the package as opposed to a generalized food chart.

There may be some tweaking to do with portions in the beginning as you adjust in response weight changes.

There is too much variance in the range of appropriate weight to specifically define the goal of every individual puppy. The best way to know relates to appearance.

Being **underweight** proves detrimental to your puppy's development as much as being overweight so pay close attention to body proportions throughout development.

Obviously, puppies should not be round. As they grow, you should be able to see an obvious waistline developing, similar to the proportions of an adult dog.

Underweight puppies, of course, will have this feature, but you shouldn't be able to count the ribs from a distance.

If you have concerns about weight, whether it's too much or not enough, check with your vet before making any big portion changes.

The Same Old Isn't Boring for Dogs

Speaking of changes, once you find a food that suits both your pup and your budget, it's okay to stick with just the one. Dogs aren't particular to variety and changing from one type of food to another can result in digestive issues, especially when the change is sudden. The puppy's system has become accustomed to the balance of nutrients in the current food, and a switch to a different formula or brand requires the system to readjust. The transition interrupts an established process.

When a diet change is unavoidable, you can help ease the transition by switching out the kibble gradually. The first day, serve meals that are 75 percent of the old food, with the new food making up the remaining 25 percent.

The next day, if your pup hasn't had any adverse reaction to the introduction of a new formula of food, increase the percentage to half old and half new.

Back off again if this causes upset. Your puppy may seem to be stable after one day of the 50/50 mix, but it is a good idea to remain with that ratio for another day or two.

The next step would be a mix of 25 percent old and 75 percent new. A day or so later, you can begin to serve full portions of the new food alone.

Keep in mind that this process needs to done every time you switch from one food to another. The process is required even if you are returning to a brand you've used in the past.

Where to Dine

Now that you have ideas about food options, you can decide where your pup will dine.

Many people keep food dishes in or near the kitchen, and there is no reason not to. Puppies are rarely bothered by the amount of traffic buzzing by them when they are hyper-focused on dinner. Getting your puppy used to eating in the midst of activity can even prove beneficial.

The high traffic could help prevent or, at least, diminish any future food-related issues.

Puppies can sometimes develop possessive behavior, often called guarding, whenever they have food, treats or bones in their custody. The causes of bad conduct vary, but one factor could involve the place where they eat most often. If the typical dining venue has been a secluded corner, or some tucked away enclave, then the pup is accustomed to eating in isolation.

If the pup suddenly finds the venue has been moved to a central location filled with activity, the dramatic change can bring on anxiety and amplify the natural aversion to meal sharing.

Now the owners are surprised that the puppy seems nervous as kibble flows into dishes. The activity used to inspire dances of mounting excitement and anticipation. They don't understand why the pup keeps watch over one shoulder and shows the pearly whites whenever anyone comes near. The undesirable behavior is common for all breeds of dogs, but the food-related growls and displays of aggression need to be addressed.

Remember the general rule is to not give attention to unwanted behavior. It is not ideal to scold or punish your pup while the growling is taking place or when the hair along its back is standing on end.

Consult with the instructor of the puppy class for ideas on curbing the conduct. Do not let the behavior continue because the possessive response will always pose a safety threat. Kids can forget that your dog is completely different in the presence of food, from friendly to snarling in mere seconds. This behavior puts everyone at risk, but children in particular due to size and proximity to the height of your dog.

Secondly, this behavior could prove hazardous every you go where treats are used regularly. This means your dog could launch into attack mode if another dog goes for his treat. Even when the food is not meant for your dog, this same protective response could create a fight.

Other instances could happen in a park, and dog parks in particular. Owners often bring bones and rawhides with them to keep the pets occupied while they rest momentarily. When partially eaten bones are left behind, your dog could happen across one and begin aggressively claiming if for himself. This proves hazardous for both people and other animals that might approach without realizing a bone has entered the equation.

You get an idea of how this behavior can create problems in various settings where your dog will spend time. Guarding food, however, is not an area where you can apply the philosophy of ignoring bad behavior. Whenever you notice any signs of aggressing, it's highly possible that you will need to step your obedience efforts.

The initial practice will require a lease and color that fits properly. If your dog is no longer a puppy, you can use a slip collar. A slip collar is typically made from a chain that has larger loops on each end. The collar is placed on the dog; the chain will be able to move through the largest link that will be attached to the leash. When you pull on the leash with a very small quick tug, the chain makes a noise that will get your dog's attention. You never want to forcefully pull on the leash or collar because the collar will tighten too much on your dog's neck.

When you have leash and collar in place on your dog, lead them over their bowl with a meal's amount of food in it.

Stand there as your dog begins to sniff or eat the food. Whenever your pup growls or bares his teeth, say "no" as you pull slightly on the leash so the chain makes a sound. You would then guide your dog away from the food, remain a distance away momentarily, and repeat the practice.

The dog might not reach the point where they don't growl in only one training session. You will need to repeat this activity whenever the behavior happens or returns.

This same method can be effective when used with other scenarios where your dog shows a protective instinct inappropriately. You will want to check with a trainer about the best approach to take before putting this method into action.

Another approach is only effective when you have effectively established your rank as pack leader. Never try to take food or bones from a dog by hand unless you have 100 percent certainty that your dog understands you are the boss.

Again, only try this method of correction after verifying with a trainer that it is an appropriate approach to take on your dog.

The reason this method is effective in the right circumstances involves canine social rules and instinct. Dog's instinctually submit to their leader of the pack, which in the domestic arena in you. You are allowed to take away the food or the bone or the treat, and when the food guarding behavior happens, do so. When the behavior has stopped, return the bowl to the floor.

A dog should be allowed to eat freely when no growling is taking place. When it does happen, however, calmly but sternly say "no" and remove the bowl from the pup's reach again. Return it to the floor when aggression dissipates. Continue to do this practice on other occasions when the behavior presents.

Again, never use this approach before an undisputed pecking order has been well established and tested.

Three Squares

The entire amount of food for one day shouldn't be dished out in one lump sum. Consider the schedule you use for daily intake. Most likely, you don't eat one meal a day. Many people no longer limit the number of times they eat to the traditional breakfast, lunch, and dinner philosophy. The trend is more like three meals plus several snack breaks.

This same idea of spacing the day's food ration into set intervals of the day provides the same benefits for dogs. Think of each portion you deliver as one of your puppies three squares for the day, spaced at a consistent amount of time apart.

By spreading out the total amount, your pup will receive a steady source of fuel and a better chance to absorb nutrients. If feasible, in the first weeks after bringing the pup home, you should divide daily food rations into four meals to keep your pup on track nutritionally. You can move to three times a day when your puppy reaches three months of age.

Again, serve only the amount of food your puppy needs per meal. Little ones love to eat, and they won't stop doing so until there's not a nugget in sight. If you serve the entire day's take at once, your pup will eat it all at once and expect more next mealtime.

The schedule for feeding can have some flexibility but remember to keep the timing suitable to your lifestyle. Your pup will quickly develop an internal dinner bell sounds when it's meal time without fail.

If you want to test the accuracy of this ability, wait until the next seasons when time shifts by an hour. Whether it's forward or back, your pup expects meals at the same time of day but will be an hour off.

With this concept in mind, you would be wise to delay serving breakfast during the work week, instead of filling your pup's bowl first thing in the morning. This simple shift will teach your puppy to expect a late breakfast instead of waking you early on Saturday morning because it's time to eat.

Space feeding times out as evenly as possible and offer the last meal of the day several hours prior to bedtime. This food break at the end of the day will help your puppy get through the night without needing a bathroom break.

For at least the first six months, continue serving three meals per day. From there on, you can divide daily calories between two meals throughout your dog's adult and senior years.
As always, there is no agreed-upon age when

dogs should transition from puppy food to adult formulas. You will often hear that a puppy reaches adulthood at the age of one and needs to switch to dog food then. This rule doesn't apply to all breeds across the board. Larger breeds, like Labs, continue growing past the age of one and often continue to require the growth support puppy food provides.

Seek advice from your veterinarian, and together, you can determine when your puppy has finished growing.

Dining In

Most of the advice from experts deal with consistency, but for meal time, feel free to mix it up in terms of location. You can get your puppy used to eating in situations where the activity and visibility levels vary.

One idea that will have twice the benefit involves your puppy's crate. If your newbie remains apprehensive about the "den," it may increase the comfort level if you occasionally make it the dining venue. This action will give your pup a positive experience to associate with time spent in the crate.

The Dishes

There aren't any set rules concerning dishes or one definitive type that has been proven superior to others. Dinnerware doesn't even have to have the original purpose for canine consumption.

If you do use a bowl from your own cabinet, choose one that can take a handle a bit of abuse. Labradors love playing with food dishes almost as much as eating from them, so this fact is something to keep in mind.

For dog-specific options, stainless steel dishes have the aspect of durability in their favor. The shiny silver bowls aren't very heavy, though, and unless they have been weighted, they are easily tipped over. Again, this scenario means playtime for Labradors, so keep in mind the noise factor when considering stainless steel bowls.

Plastic dishes remain readily available, and to reduce the tipping-ability factor, some manufacturers offer bowls with various weight options. While plastic obviously makes much less commotion as it rolls down the hallway, you need to pay attention to the quality of the plastic. Not all pet food dishes come free of materials reported as toxic. If an item is BPA-free, it will typically have a statement on the packaging to market that aspect of the product.

Other options include a variety of ceramic and glass. Regardless of material, make sure the bowls are weighted for stability and durable enough to withstand a dog with a strong mouthing instinct.

Finding and Visiting the Veterinarian

In addition to proper nutrition, preventative health care can help your puppy stay well and free from parasites.

The first step involves finding a good vet that suits both you and your dog. You'll want a professional who takes time not only with your puppy but with you as well. A good veterinarian will offer full explanations for test results, inoculations, recommended products, and any necessary follow-up care. You should feel like the vet understands and responds fully to your questions and concerns.

To find the right match, ask around. Personal recommendations remain a top method of finding any service, including health care providers for your pet.

The most honest and reliable recommendations come from people who have experience with a provider. Whether the experience was good or bad, the information will help direct you accordingly.

Ask friends, coworkers, the instructor in your puppy class and even people you meet at the dog park. When you notice a name repeated more often than others, it's a good bet that you should start with the most popular choice. Current clients can provide helpful information about their favored vet, but it can also be helpful to know where NOT to go too. People will gladly share stories of bad experiences they had with a certain doctor or at a particular animal clinic.

You might not want to automatically eliminate a vet based on only one opinion. However, when you hear the same name repeatedly, followed by a statement like, "never go there," it's probably a good idea to never go there.

Other methods of finding a good vet involve calling around. Typically, a good vet is a busy one. If you call for a first-time appointment, and the doctor's schedule is wide open, you'll be wise to pick the next name on your list of potentials.

On the flip side, you don't want to wait several weeks or more for an appointment. Odds are you'll need to make future appointments far in advance. This proves problematic when health concerns arise suddenly, or your pup has been injured. You'll want a doctor willing to work you into the schedule for urgent matters. Otherwise, you would need to make a costly visit to the nearest emergency vet clinic.

The next item to note involves the reception you receive when you make your first call to an office. The staff should seem friendly, polite, and responsive to your questions. If you are put on hold immediately, remember it's a good sign for the office to be busy. However, if the person answering doesn't ask to put you on hold before sending you there, there is a lack of professionalism. If you are ever left on hold or if various people pick up, ask a question, then return you to hold, it's a sign the office is understaffed. An office that does not have enough people to professionally receive calls typically rushes clients through all other services or keeps people waiting well past the time of their appointment. Either way, the quality of care suffers.

When you find a vet that seems like a good match, you can verify the suitability in several ways during the first visit.

The most important factor concerns your puppy's comfort level. It's common for animals to show signs of anxiety whenever they go into a vet's office. There are a plethora of sounds, smells, and activities that can easily overwhelm your dog's keen senses. The important thing to notice concerns the interactions between the doctor and your dog. Does the vet have a calm demeanor upon entering the exam room? Dogs quickly pick up on emotions, and they will feel more at ease with a doctor who isn't stressed and working hurriedly.

Vets should be cordial to both the owner and the patient. They should introduce themselves as the first order of business, and then extend the friendly greeting to your puppy. When a vet addresses your pet by name, you will know they took the time to at least glance at the chart.

Your puppy will probably seem nervous

throughout the visit, but the doctor should know methods of interaction that can ease some apprehension.

Dogs really do have an instinct for judging character, so make sure your pup takes a liking to the vet. In the first part of the visit, a good vet will ask if you have any immediate concerns. The next item should involve an explanation of what will take place during the examination and the reason for each service.

First Visit Procedures

Putting your puppy on the scale to check weight and height

During the exam, the vet should specifically check ears, eyes, nose, gums, teeth, pads of the paws, and genitalia. This is in addition to a general overall assessment of your pup's proportions and the appearance of the coat and skin.

The doctor will also get a temperature and listen through a stethoscope for a regular heartbeat and clear breathing.

The physical portion of the exam should also include applying gentle pressure on various areas of the belly, abdomen, and lymph nodes. This procedure will ensure there are no painful areas or unusual lumps that would prompt concern.

Fecal and urine samples will be processed through the lab during your visit, and most likely, the doctor will leave the room momentarily to review the outcome.

Puppies from reputable breeders will have had the first round of vaccines prior to going home with new owners. These are shots due at six weeks of age.

You should have received health records from the breeder listing all health-related care that your puppy received during the six to eight weeks of life.

The vet will review these records to determine the procedures required for the first visit.

Between the ages of six to eight weeks, puppies are able to have vaccines to cover **distemper, parainfluenza,** and **bordetella**.

The next round of shots is due between ten to twelve weeks of age and include **DHPP**, **adenovirus**, and **parvovirus**. A **rabies** shot can be given when your puppy is twelve weeks or older.

Remember, these vaccines are recommended and not mandatory, with the exception of rabies.

Be sure to check laws governing your area concerning this vaccination. In many areas of the United States, rabies vaccination is required by law. Some states don't require the vaccine at all, while others have laws that pertain to dogs but not cats.

For the recommended vaccines, do your own research before deciding on the ones you feel are necessary for your puppy. If there are any inoculations, you can forgo for your particular situation will mean fewer injections for your pet and a lower cost for you.

You can discuss any vaccine-related concerns with your vet, as well as ask for advice on which ones are not necessary for your circumstances. For example, if you don't plan to have your puppy in a kennel situation, doggie daycare, or any place where exposure to other dogs is high, you can choose to skip the vaccine for a kennel cough. Remember, though, you need to discuss the issue thoroughly with your vet before making final decisions.

Many experts agree on the importance of guarding your dog against two dangerous diseases that have severe and potentially fatal consequences.

Canine Distemper is a highly contagious virus that dogs can contract in three main situations. The virus can be passed from a contaminated surface or object as well as direct contact with an infected animal. Even more concerning is the fact that the disease can also be passed through the air. The virus affects the respiratory system.

Distemper can be scary, considering there is currently no known cure. Vaccinations remain the best way to protect against the disease.

The virus is related to the measles, which is the reason you might see a vaccination listed this way on a schedule of canine vaccinations.

The second vaccine experts highly recommend combats the potentially fatal canine parvovirus. This disease, more commonly known as parvo, passes through direct and indirect contact with the virus. Once infected, the virus mainly affects the gastrointestinal system.

If your puppy is due for vaccines, the vet should let you know the name of each vaccination and the reason for it before moving forward with a round of shots. Remember, most vaccines are optional, so you will want to know which ones are necessary for your particular situation.

When it's time to administer the vaccines, some vets take the animals to the back room for injections, while others give the shots in the exam room while you are present.

The location is typically a matter of doctor preference, but if you prefer one way over the other, the vet should be accommodating.

Spaying and Neutering

Unless you have expert-level knowledge about breeding and caring for pre-weaned puppies, you should not consider letting your pet reproduce. One exception involves competition. Show dogs are required to remain unaltered when they are in formal shows sponsored by organizations such as AKC. For this requirement, you'd need to forgo having your dog spayed or neutered until retirement age.

Otherwise, the health benefits of having your puppy fixed outweigh any drawbacks of having a successful spaying or neutering procedure.

Talk to your vet about cost and other concerns you have. If there are financial issues, some doctors offer payment plans or know sources for subsidized options.

Many areas have organizations that provide low-cost spaying and neutering services. Other affordable options can be set up through local animal shelters as well. You can publications covering your community for information about such services or check through the database of providers of subsidized spaying and neutering procedures. In some states, the services are provided free of cost through funding from the American Society for the Prevention of Cruelty to Animals. ASPCA is an organization that helps protect, rescue and place animals. You can check its database of low-cost spaying and neutering service with this link to their site: https://www.aspca.org/pet-care/general-pet-care/low-cost-spayneuter-programs.

The list of benefits from spaying and neutering involve help with prevention of some serious diseases, including types of cancer and infections specific to reproduction. These diseases often prove fatal for half of the animals affected.

For male dogs, they will be less likely to wander far from home. They will prefer to remain safe at home with their pack instead of getting lost in unfamiliar territory or wandering through high-traffic areas. Altered males also tend to display better behavior than unneutered dogs.

There are more benefits that result from having female dogs fixed also. In addition to health-related pluses, there will be no heat cycle requiring extra care. That also means you also won't have runaway male dogs hanging around your house either.

The bottom line is, altered pets typically live

longer and tend to be better behaved.

The Price of Health

Spaying and neutering procedures are the only expense you'll face trying to ensure your pup stays healthy.

The cost of health care overall can add up quickly, so it could be worthwhile to research payment options.

Financing

Taking the necessary precautions to ensure the health of your pup is expensive, but it's not an ideal place in the budget to cut costs. When bills get hard to handle, ask your vet about payment options. With the high cost of some procedures, financing has become more and more necessary.

Credit cards issued specially for pet-related costs are another way to finance medical bills. CareCredit offers a card that provides payment options for all vet care, including routine visits, spaying procedures, and emergencies.

Health Insurance

Pet Plan boasts high ratings from both pet experts and pet owners alike. There are plans with varying deductibles, with high options amounted to lower premiums. There are no age limitations, but rates do change according to the age of the pet.

In addition to sudden illnesses and accidents, the coverage extends to hereditary and predisposed conditions as well as chronic ailments.

Larger breeds are typically predisposed to a condition called hip dysplasia, which is specifically mentioned in coverage options.

Other options include plans covering dental issues, prescription medication, and alternative therapy.
Nationwide and Healthy Paws are two more pet insurance providers to compare when shopping for coverage to suits your needs.

When you must curb actual costs but don't want to put your pup at risk, you can look into vaccination clinics. A recent movement to make vet care more affordable for pet owners involves scheduled times and places where a local veterinarian will be onsite to provide low-cost vaccinations. These events are often advertised in newspapers and local independent publications, especially those focusing on pets.

More Preventative Considerations

Vets frequently bring up the issue of **heartworm** automatically, but if not, be sure to ask. This disease comes from infected mosquitoes that pass the worm into the bloodstream while in the process of drawing blood from a dog. The worms then make their way toward the heart, and once there, they start to reproduce. Initial infection typical remains symptom-free, but over time, as the number of worms increases, the health of the pet deteriorates.

Each yearly checkup should include a blood test to check for heartworm infection. Catching the condition early will help minimize the extent of treatment for the infection. Early detection can also improve the odds for your dog's full recovery.

Prevention is simple, and the most popular option comes in a once-a-month chewable tablet that your pup will consider a treat. Some brands have the added benefit of flea protection. Heartworm treatments can also come in the form of a topical solution or be administered by injection.

The cost of prevention, regardless of the option you choose, averages out to $10 per month. Heartworm infections have been reported in all areas of the United States.

Fleas

Fleas are jumping insects that feed on the blood of animals, including you. Their bite can cause an allergic reaction that could drive your puppy to chew relentlessly at the site of the bite. An allergic reaction, called moist dermatitis, can result in infected and inflamed areas on the body. The lesions, commonly called hot spots, start off as self-inflicted areas where incessant scratching, licking, and chewing have caused hair loss and breaks in skin surfaces. The inflamed areas can become infected and very painful

Typically, the problem begins at the site of flea bites in patches near the tail, top of the legs, and sides of the chest. Other areas can become a problem, though, and it's not uncommon for bald spots to appear anywhere within where biting, licking, or scratching reach.

There are many over the counter products available to treat hot spots, but your vet can suggest the best options for your dog.

Control

Fleas reproduce quickly and prove to be quite resilient. To rid your home and pet of fleas takes effort and persistence once infestation takes hold. The resolution should be a multifaceted effort involving flea baths, topical flea treatment applications, and ongoing maintenance with prevention products. Your home could require some type of flea "bomb" and then a thorough cleaning to remove fleas and eggs.

Tapeworm infestation is another health issue to watch for whenever your dog incurs a flea problem. Fleas can carry tapeworm eggs, and when a dog chews on an itchy bite, there is a risk of consuming that flea.

When this situation occurs, the dog then becomes a host for the parasite. Make sure, whenever you have an issue with fleas, to watch for any small white particles in your dog's feces. Tapeworms shed body segments that are excreted by your dog. Often, these segments will appear to be live worms as the pieces continue to move after being shed.

Again, consult your veterinarian about the issue. The doctor can check a fecal sample for evidence of a tapeworm and provide an effective treatment. Over-the-counter products are available for deworming, but using such products without advice from your vet is risky.

As mentioned before, some heartworm medications also protect against fleas. Another option for keeping your dog flea free is a monthly application of a liquid form of flea repellant.

Frontline and **K9 Advantix** offer topical products to help prevent both fleas and ticks. A small amount of the liquid solution comes in a sealed applicator. Every month, one applicator of solution is typically applied in a line starting between the shoulder blades to the base of the tail. Every product varies, so be sure to read instructions fully before using pest control products. A package with six applications costs between $45 to $60.

There are also chewable tablets, such as **Nexgar**, that are also made to kill and repel fleas. These too are given once a month, and price varies according to weight. The average cost is $45 for three chews.

Traditional products, like flea collars and sprays, remain on the market but have rarely provide full and lasting protection from fleas.

Just when you think you have all the medical issues under control, there's a sudden illness or injury that occurs. These are rarely timed conveniently, it seems. When an emergency arises after hours, an emergency pet clinic will be the place to go. Often, pet ERs are open at night and on weekends when regular vets are off the clock. This is a lifesaving option, no question, but you can expect the bill to be at least 30 percent higher than standard vet charges. Fortunately, most will accept insurance and pet care credit cards.

Be sure to have information on the nearest **emergency pet clinic** readily available. You can keep the phone number and address on your refrigerator so you won't waste time searching during an emergency situation.

Grooming and Other Fun Ways to Bond

Despite their minimal fur length and typically matte-free coat, Labradors do require regular grooming. Most likely, your pup will be happy with the shower of attention that comes with brushing and smoothing, especially if you introduce the activity early on in puppyhood. Remember that Labs have a thick dense coat, and shedding remains constant all year long. Their fur may be short, but there are multiple layers, and these layers produce a large amount of hair. While you can expect a lot of shedding, frequent brushing will help keep dog hair out of your living space, or at least to a minimum.

Some form of brushing, combing, or raking will

be necessary at least weekly. Excessive amounts of dead hair can cause discomfort for your pup, so professional groomers often recommend a quick daily brush out or at least a three-times-per-week routine. All brushes are not created equal, and like all other necessities, you will find an ample variety of combs, brushes, rakes, and so on.

A firm **bristled brush** will smooth fur and help to disperse the oils that support healthy skin and shiny fur. The firmness can also loosen mud, dirt, or other debris from their fur. This will prove a useful aspect for grooming your pup because Labs tend to gravitate toward areas where muck is plentiful.

In addition to bristle brushes, groomers frequently use a tool called a **slicker brush** during low shedding seasons. This device had a flat head covered with wire bristles and a straight ergonomic handle. The price and quality range extend from one end of the spectrum to the other. As the standard goes, the price represents the level of quality, and for a slicker brush, be wary of the cheap ones. You don't want to run low grade, wire bristles against your dog's the skin, especially if all the rows of wires aren't the same height. Cheaper brushes generally have sharper wires and pose the risk of injury.

Professional quality slicker brushes cost an average of $25 to $30. For that price, the wire bristles should feel very smooth, somewhat soft, and be positioned in the unified surface level.

You can plan to spend around $15 for mid-range quality, and some cheaper brushes cost less than $5.

Combs with a widely spread metal teeth can also help remove average amounts of shedding, but neither a slicker nor a comb can handle the amount of hair that is released as warmer weather approaches.

What Big Hair You Have

The process ramps up in volume every year as summer approaches. Rising temperatures render the undercoat unnecessary, and it vacates in mass quantities. This time of year will definitely require adamant bouts with the brush.

But whenever summer approaches each year, the hair comes loose in unbelievable amounts.

One of the most helpful tools to combat the fur storm is a rake-style gadget called the **FURminator Deshedding** Tool for Dogs by Professional Pet Products.

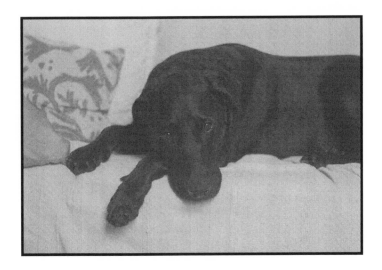

The manufacturer offers several options, each geared toward breed size and length of the coat.

For Labradors, choose the tool labeled short-hair. The first look at the rake-like device can fool you. It has a tight row of short teeth along the length of the rake head that doesn't look like they'd break the surface of the coat, let alone battle the shedding.

But somehow, it does work—and very well. The

manufacturer claims regular brushing, with the FURminator, for instance, three times per week, can take care of up to 90 percent of the loose hair.

Every time you use the tool, even in other seasons, you will wonder where the massive amounts of hair you removed had been stored. Your dog won't look slimmer, so the mystery remains.

The newest feature tool is the FURjector button helps release hair from the device, allowing for easy cleaning. Prices for the FURminators range from $24 to $38.

Be advised, though, that it's best to brush with a deshedder tool outside simply due to the mass amount of hair that it extracts.

Lastly, you could find some deshedding tools

with the combination of a rake and some form of blade incorporated into one device. The safe use of these gadgets has been a topic of controversy, and most experts advise against using the tool for at home grooming efforts.

Options When the Fur Flies

If you are new the issue of shedding, you could be shocked by the amount of fur that comes loose when molting season hits. You will need to step up the grooming efforts to minimize the amount of dead hair that would otherwise wind up on your furniture and rugs.

There are alternatives available that can assist when shedding reaches an all-time high.

First of all, you can take your lab to a professional groomer for a thorough removal of dead hair. This process, of course, won't bring an end to future shedding, so subsequent trips would be in order.

The cost depends on the amount of work needed to get your dog looking good, but you can expect to pay a base price of $45–$50.

For a less expensive option, look for self-service salons where you can bring your pup in and do the work yourself. Most places have groomers to assist throughout the process as needed. This venue might be helpful at other times too, especially after your lab has been out doing what Labs do, such as rolling in the smelliest spots they can find or chasing the smelliest critters. Do-it-yourself salons offer a myriad of fixes, from high-powered hoses and scented shampoos to disinfecting baths and de-skunking soaks. The basic services starting at $10 each.

Tips for Grooming Resistant Dogs

The number one tip for getting a dog used to grooming is to make the experience as fun and positive as possible, especially for dogs who avert brushes baths and trims and cleaning.

As with all activities that dogs resist, it is best to prepare for grooming challenges as early as possible. Grooming can increase the bond between owner and animal, but negative experiences definitely cause setbacks for all concerned.

To get a pet used to the activity, start gently and keep the practice regular. Labradors are fairly low maintenance when it comes to grooming due to their short coat. A regular even daily brushing helps minimize issues with shedding. Remember to up the amount of time spent on brushing when temperatures start rising because Labs tend to shed their undercoat, which can result in a lot of hair loss.

For the first groom, it's best not to simply dive into the task. A pup needs time to build trust and face new experiences. One simple trick to ease anxiety involves inspection. Show the dog the tools that will soon be running over the length of the body. Let the dog nudge, sniff, paw, or any safe way the pup uses to make sure the instrument won't pose a threat.

After this introduction, put the tools aside and start again the next day with the introduction and begin gently brushing. Keep the experience short if the dog appears apprehensive. It is essential that the owner remain calm and upbeat throughout the entire process. Dogs pick up on emotions, good and bad, and will follow the owner's lead accordingly.

Bathing at Home

At home, you won't have to wash your dog often, unless smell or dirt is an obvious issue. Bathing too frequently can strip away too much of the oils needed to maintain healthy skin and a shiny coat.

Your puppy doesn't need daily bathing. In fact, bathing frequently can strip away the oils that protect the skin from dryness and irritations. But there are times when your muddy pup will need some attention.

When you do bathe your dog, both during puppyhood and as an adult, use lukewarm water and a mild shampoo. Never use your own shampoo or any products made for people, even the cleanser intended for babies. Ingredients used for those formulas, if you get any in your dog's eyes, it will result in burning or stinging sensations. Your dog will then associate bathing with a painful experience, making the task more challenging in the future.

When the doggy odor is an issue and you want to use shampoo with fragrance, try to avoid cleansers with strong scents that are made with artificial fragrances. Your dog a strong sense of smell so you don't want to overwhelm the senses, and also the chemical perfumes can sometimes cause dryness and skin irritation. Look for natural scents, such as pure lavender oil, and cleanses that are pH balanced.

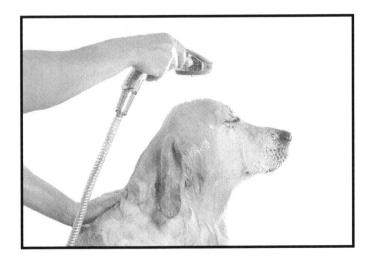

You can bathe your Lab once a month without too much concern for oil loss if you use a natural and gentle cleanser.

Puppies don't necessarily need to be bathed unless they become mucked covered, but you can give them a pre-bath experience using water only. If the cleanser is necessary, though, use the same rules mentioned previously concerning all-natural products. You will also need to find a formula made specifically for puppies. This introduction to bathing during puppyhood will help prepare both of you for bathing efforts when your dog is full grown.

The Dog Days of Summer

During warmer seasons when your pup has been romping through water or rolling around in mud, muck or worse, it's fine to spray them down with the water from the outside hose. Your Lab will welcome cold water to fend off the summer heat.

Hosing them down outside will keep dirt from coming inside. Because Labs have a water-repellent coat, you may have to massage areas where the water is beading up instead of penetrating the fur. When the hose water alone won't take care of all the dirt and odor, you can always add an environmentally friendly dog shampoo into the mix. You will need to put some effort into getting the shampoo lathered up, again due to the water-repellant quality of their coat. Most likely, you'll need to rinse and repeat to get your dog thoroughly clean.

Lastly, it's a good idea to at least towel-dry after the bath, even if you intend to let your pup dry in the sun. Soaking up at least part of the water will speed the process avoid attracting insects with prolonged dampness.

The Nails

Don't mess with the feet. That is every dog's response to nail trimming. It is rare to find any type of canine that willingly hands over a paw when its pedicure time.

Nail trimming and pad checking are tricky activities to perform due to the survival instinct. Dogs need their feet to all things related to staying alive, according to the genes passed down from their ancestors. Feet have to chase down meals, get us out of harm's way, dig holes to sleep in, dig holes to bury food, and to mark the path that leads home.

The protective instinct also results from glands in the pads that provide the dog's scent. Either as a way to mark a trail or to take ownership of an area. It's common to see a dog flinging grass and dirt around after elimination, and this gland is responsible for that behavior. It's all about scent.

Begin Foot Work Early

You can work to desensitize your puppy's feet, and the earlier you get started, the better chance you'll have when you try to trim the nails of your full-grown adult dog. When spending time with the young Labrador during downtime, start petting calmly and then work toward the feet.

Try gently massaging around the ankle area then move to holding a paw with one thumb and gently rubbing in a slow circular motion on the top of the foot.

You might have to gradually go through small steps of this procedure and progress a little further each day. If your dog becomes defensive at one stage, back off. You need to spend more time at the place of comfort. Once a dog is comfortable with someone touching and gently holding the paw, an owner can begin working with the pads of the feet. This is also a good time to check the feet to make sure there are no injuries or cracks to the pads. You should also check for debris between the toes.

Working regularly with a puppy's feet will prove beneficial but nail clipping remains one of the more daunting tasks of grooming. The procedure is rarely a simple process, but when a dog is less protective over its means for survival, a dramatic wrestling match won't ensue.

Speaking of nail trimming, it is essential to keep the nails from growing out too long. Aside from the obvious reason, there is the problem of the quick lengthening as the nail grows.

The **quick,** or technically the **hyponychium**, is the tissue at the base of the nail and the blood source as well. You want to avoid the quick, but it's not always easy. Labs typically have dark nails that make quicks difficult to pinpoint and easy to nip with the clippers. The immediate negatives are pain for your dog and excessive bleeding from the injury.

Future trims can be more challenging too because the dog now has a negative association with nail trimming.

It happens, though, to amateurs as well as professionals. If it does, you should try to remain calm so your puppy won't feel stressed. You will next want to stop the bleeding. Sometimes there could be a lot of bleeding, but it should respond to a **blood-clotting agent**. Some people keep styptic pens on hand for this purpose. The pens contain silver nitrate that will effectively stop the bleeding. If you don't have one, you can make your own clotter by mixing cornstarch and water to form a paste. When that is ready you can apply a small amount directly on the bleeding nail using a Q-tip or edge of a tissue. There is no need to wipe the blood away before applying. Leave the concoction on the nail for several minutes. If the bleeding hasn't subsided, you can add some more paste to the nail.

Typically, the bleeding will stop on its own. If you have concerns about the length of time that the bleeding persists, be sure to contact your vet.

Even when the bleeding has stopped, you should try to keep your dog from excessive activity that could put pressure on the injury. You should aim for thirty minutes, but any length of low activity would prove helpful. If the activity is too intense too soon, putting pressure on the foot could cause the bleeding to resume.

The ears can be tricky to clean too. This is mainly due to your dog's keen sense of hearing. The sound of solution filling their ears can become overwhelming and worrisome to them.

The best first approach is to make sure you show them the tools. They can sniff and inspect all they want, but make sure all products are tightly sealed for this activity.

The approach professionals take involves taking a liquid ear cleaner and filling the ear. This is not recommended for dog owners to do at home, especially when the practice is new to both you and your dog. You can start by squirting some of the solution on a cotton ball and then gently squeezing some liquid from the cotton ball into the ear. If the dog is open to the idea, you can use the cotton ball to gently wipe the outer portion of the ear well. Never stick any type of utensil into your dog's ear, whether you are trying to clean or clear out wax. That is a job to leave for your next visit to the vet. Typically, you can do the cotton ball trick and that will take care of any average, day to day issues.

Remember to give your dog some room because as soon as the liquid goes into the ear, your dog will start shaking it out. Shaking the solution out is the best way to finish the job cleaning. But you don't want to be in the way of any airborne solution. After the shaking is all through, you can dry your dog's ears with a soft towel. It is better to soak up some of the dampness because the top of the outer ear will flop over and impede the drying process. The floppy ear and dampness are one of the main reasons cleaning is necessary in the first place.

Cleaning could help prevent ear infections, so if your dog is prone to infections, you would want to keep this a part of the regular routine. Washing ears too often, however, can cause irritation.

The frequency of ear cleaning is another topic to discuss with your vet. Your dog's specific health history will help the doctor provide advice to suit your pup.

Another method for knowing when to clean the ears involves smell, meaning, there shouldn't be any. The emission of a foul odor rising from the ear canal can signal an infection. That not always the case, but it is a possibility. One sign of possible infection could be the color of wax you see when you look into the ear. Remember not to use any type of instrument to do this. Lift your dog's ear and look in with the naked eye only. If you notice black or dark-colored "gunk," the ears could be infected. When in doubt, make an appointment to see the vet.

If the at-home method isn't sufficient to erase odor, a groomer can also do a more thorough job. There should not be any medical issues when you use a groomer as an option for ear cleanings.

Bathing Alternatives and Tub Assistance

During the colder months when indoor bathing is a must, a bathtub isn't the only option for grooming. There are devices called portable pet showers that you can use, and these are a good idea for pet owners living in homes that have only shower stalls. The device, however, can be used in other areas of the home, not simply bathrooms.

Think of the way a carpet cleaner operates. There is a reservoir for water and soap and a means for dispersing the mix over the area being cleaned. Directly after application of the solution, a vacuum-like component then sucks dirt and used water back into a separate storage tank. This is the operation that takes place with a portable pet shower.

One of the top sellers is **Bissell's BarkBath grooming systems**. There are various options for capacity and prices range from $50 for the smallest system. The system recommended for sixty- to eighty-pound dogs costs around $150.

If you already have a carpet cleaner, however, there is a tool you can purchase that serves as an attachment. An example is **Bissell's BarkBath Dog Grooming Tool** for Portable Carpet Cleaners. The tool comes with rinse-free dog shampoo, like the other full systems. The average sale price is $45, although the list price is $70.

If you would rather use a tub, but find it challenging to reach all areas of your dog while stooped over one side of the bath, a Booster Bath could help. The product is a plastic tub on legs that attaches to a water source with one hose and a second hose works as a drain. The item includes accessories to hold shampoo bottles and secure your pet inside the tub. This design gives you access to your pup from all sides and you do all the work from a standing position. One helpful that is available but not included is a set of compatible steps. The tub is elevated and the steps would save you from having to lift a full-grown lab two to three feet from the ground.

What to Do for Fun

After you have your pup looking his best, you can strengthen your bond even more with some fun together time. One of the best ways to bond with your dog involves investing in quality time, especially when that time is spent playing.

Labs are content with all things running, jumping, swimming, and high-energy oriented. But you might not be.

So what activities can suit both of your interests?

You can begin with any activity that lets your Lab do what Labs do best-retrieve. Your dog will most likely stay entertained with games of fetch, from chasing toy ducks to catching frisbees. This type of activity will give them the necessary exercise while not expending all of your energy.

Be sure, however, that the toys you choose pose no health or safety issues for your pup.

Balls that bounce make a good tool for many games. One in particular involves you hurling the ball against an outside wall letting your retriever retrieve it. Tennis balls are good for this game, but not if they are poor quality or made with toxic materials.

The best way to ensure the toys are dog-friendly

involves finding ones that are made specifically for pets. Kong air dog and hyper pet are examples of tennis ball toys available at pet stores.

The same idea holds for games of Frisbee. Your dog would probably run to catch every throw, despite repeated injuries incurred each time the hard plastic hits the mouth. To avoid dental damage and still keep the game, you can invest in **soft-bite Frisbees** like flippy flopper by Hyper Pets or Boodas Soft Bite Turbo Flyer.

One game that trainers advise against is the traditional game of tug-of-war. You could be very tempted to the take the lead from your dog when he pushes the end of the rope toward your hand but keeps the other end clenched between his teeth. This is a common behavior that occurs frequently during puppyhood. Don't be fooled by the playful look and wagging tail. This game is not just for fun. It's a friendly competition where canines can prove their strength. There are plenty of dog toys made with rope that are can soothe the mouthing instinct, but you shouldn't use these in the way your dog tries to persuade you to do.

If you accept the challenge and lose to your dog, meaning the rope slips from your hand and your pup still an end gripped in his mouth, you could lose your position as pack leader.

Even worse, when this situation occurs during puppyhood, it could thwart the efforts you have made to establish the pecking order of the pack. You should keep your dog aligned with the idea that you are the pack leader and all other human members of the family higher on the ladder of command that the dog. If you fail to prove your superior strength, your dog will no longer consider you unbeatable. This is not a good position for a pack leader. The shift in power could dampen quick responses to your commands. And the more losses you have, the less respect you can expect. This response is not always apparent, but undoubtedly, you will no longer seem all powerful from your dog's point of view.

Aside from fun and games together, there will be situations when your dog is home alone.

When you're not around to provide entertainment, you'll need to find an activity for your pup to do in your absence. You can take advantage of your Lab's food obsession with toys made to hold their attention. After all, a bored, energetic, intelligent dog rarely does anything productive.

While the Owner's Away

Interactive toys can help ease issues that come from boredom. Slo-Bowl by Outward Hound is one option that could keep your pup focused on dinner. The instead of the traditional bowl with a single surface to hold food, the Slo-Bowl has a maze of circular and rows that require some interaction before the food comes loose. The dog needs to nose and nuzzle the kibble loose, and this effort will hold their interest longer than the typical time a meal would take.

Other options hold treats inside balls or cubes, and as your dog noses the objects around, pieces of treat fall through a hole. The treats come out sparingly so keep the dog playing to get more.

Treats can also be hidden in stabilized puzzles that require a dog to paw and nose moveable parts to gain access to the food.

There are non-food-oriented puzzle options that could provide entertainment without the added calories. One such option is the **Outward Hound Hide-a-Squirrel Puzzle Toy. The puzzle looks like a plush log with holes that contain stuffed animals. If your puppy likes things that squeak, especially of the squirrel persuasion, this could be a good fit.**

Heredity and the Senior Years

W hen your dog reaches the halfway mark of the projected life expectancy, you can assume the senior years are not far. As your dog gets older, you can also assume some age-related health issues will arise.

In fact, when your dog turns five years old, the risk of developing breed-specific conditions begins to climb.

There are breed-specific disorders, which means your dog has the potential to develop certain health issues simply by being a Labrador retriever. Heritage is a contributing factor for some conditions, and other disorders are specific to larger breeds of dogs.

One serious condition Labs are prone to develop is commonly called **bloat**. It is essential for lab owners to know the first signs of this disorder because it's one that can quickly turn fatal.

Technically, the name for this stomach condition is Gastric Dilation-Volvulus or **GDV**. Other terms you might hear for this same disorder are twisting or torsion of the stomach and gastric torsion. These terms define the complications that could develop in the late stages of GDV.

The multiple terms are used for the same disorder due to the possible stages of progression.

Initially, there is stomach expansion with the occurrence of gastric dilation. At this stage, the expansion allows space for air to accumulate, and this ballooning action of the stomach presses against the diaphragm as well as nearby organs. At this point of development, you would notice your dog having some level of breathing difficulty. Another issue that occurs here that produces less obvious outward signs is a reduced flow of blood going to the heart.

The expansion creates an opportunity for the stomach twist. This stage of the disorder is called volvulus. Think of the movement as one area of the stomach starting to revolve while other areas do not. Without intervention, the contortion leads to a blockage or complete obstruction of blood flow. At this point, there is a diminutive chance for successful treatment.

The first symptom of GDV that most obviously presents is bloating. This expansion causes an extremely distended stomach, much more than the look of a belly bulging from too much food.

A dog in the beginning stages of GDV will appear upset and restless. You might notice signs of anxiety or discomfort, and often dogs at this stage will begin pacing back and forth. Shortness of breath usually becomes noticeable s as this phase progresses. A dog at this stage could go through the motions of vomiting without expelling anything, liquid or solid.

If the condition enters the second stage, the dog would demonstrate labored breathing, and the gums begin to turn pale. The pacing will stop as the dog becomes weaker, until becoming unable to walk at all. Without treatment, the condition deteriorates rapidly.

Early treatment provides the best chance for survival. If you think your dog is showing signs of bloat, don't hesitate to get an evaluation. When the condition progresses and twisting of the stomach occurs, the odds of survival drop dramatically.

The average survival rate of dogs treated for GDV is around 70 percent.

Knowing the symptoms of GDV can save your dog's life, but one question about the condition remains. Why does bloating occur in the first place? There are many theories about the root cause, but no solid evidence has confirmed indisputable triggers. Despite the lack of concrete proof, some correlating factors were noted during a five-year study of two thousand dogs.

Symptoms of GDV

- Severely distended stomach
- Nervous, unsettled behavior
- Pacing
- Unsuccessful attempts to vomit
- Labored breathing
- Pacing
- Collapse

One finding showed variances in relation to the amount of time dogs took to eat the same amount of food. The condition presented 15 percent less often in dogs that ate slowly compared to others that were speedy eaters.

Another factor relating to food involves the number of meals. Dogs that received all of the day's rations in one feeding demonstrated a higher incidence than dogs that had the day's ratios divided into two meals per day.

Temperament was also a factor that provided notable differences. Dogs with anxiety or aggression issues developed GDV more often than dogs with even temperaments. A similar result occurred for dogs in a stressful environment versus those in calm surroundings. Stressors appeared to increase the odds for GDV.

Some claims say the risk of GDV is higher when dogs drink too much water along with their food and also when dogs are exercised to close to dinner time. These theories have no backing from proof, but there is no consequence from avoiding both situations.

Labs tend to be lumpy. And the older they get, the more likely they are to develop **benign cysts and tumors**. Don't be alarmed if you happen across a random lump or two at some point during your dog's lifetime. Do, however, have each growth checked out by your vet to rule out malignancy. The majority of lumps turn out to be harmless fatty tumors called lymphomas, but the likelihood of cancer becomes greater with age. If you find a new lump in a senior dog, be sure to visit the vet as soon as you're able. Early detection of malignancies greatly improves the odds of recovery.

The main factors that reduce the possibility of most disorders also help ward off the increased risks that come with age. A lifelong mix of proper diet, daily exercise, and preventative care will help your dog make the most of the senior years.

Joint issues such as **arthritis** and **hip**

dysplasia also increase in likelihood as your lab ages. Both disorders can inhibit the full range of motion and cause varying levels of pain. These conditions can surface at any age, but the senior years hold a greater risk for development.

Arthritis can be the culprit when your dog shows signs of pain and discomfort, especially when moving from a downward position to standing. The same signs could appear following bouts of exercise that involve walking, running and particularly jumping. While the movement may seem to increase mobility at first, there will be more signs of stiffness afterward. Your dog might lick areas where there is pain, so this behavior should be noted if it happens consistently.

If you notice any limping, or your dog favoring one side more than another, have your vet take a look. There are treatments available that can bring relief. During the visit for evaluation, the doctor will typically study the way your dog moves, with displays of both slow and fast walking when possible. The doctor will also gently move limbs manually to find any joints that are suspect. This procedure uses extents of flexion and extension of the joints as problem indicators. Next, x-rays will typically be taken to gain a full scope of problem areas. In some cases, the vet will extract fluid from the joint to test for any underlying conditions, such as infection.

Arthritis can develop due to changes in the joints, most likely where cartilage has become thin or damaged. Without a smooth surface for cushioning, bones in a joint rub directly against one another, causing inflammation. The disorder can worsen as friction from movement causes bone growth around the joint. This further complication, called degenerative joint disease, can greatly increase your dog's level of pain and immobility.

The causes of arthritis can vary, but typically the condition arises from injuries or deformities that create joint instability.

When a dog is diagnosed with arthritis, there are many treatments available for improving the condition. The foremost plan of action involves diet changes for overweight dogs. Slimming down will lighten the load and alleviate excess pressure on the joints. Adding in exercise will help improve mobility, but the type of fitness needs to suit the condition of the joints. For water-loving labs, swimming is ideal.

Additional options include therapeutic level bedding and long-term pain medications. Your vet will be able to put together a plan that suits the needs and abilities of your dog.

Signs of pain and decreased range of motion could also indicate a disorder called hip dysplasia that targets large sized dogs more often than smaller breeds.

The condition occurs when the ball and socket joint of the hip doesn't form properly. Like arthritis, the bones rub together directly causing friction. As the bones continue to grind together instead of moving smoothly, the joints steadily deteriorate, often to the point of complete immobility.

The disorder causes severe pain and undoubtedly an extremely low quality of life for a dog with this affliction.

During an evaluation for hip dysplasia, the vet will perform an evaluation similar to the one done for arthritis. The initial therapy for hip dysplasia follows the same regimen as well—weight loss and low impact exercise.

Anti-inflammatory medication can bring some comfort, and your vet might suggest surgery. The mix of appropriate therapies and treatments depend on the needs and condition of each dog in particular. Your vet can advise on suitable options.

Hip Dysplasia involves heredity more than environmental conditions, but experts agree that lifestyle can affect the odds. Dogs that receive the right balance of nutrition, especially during the first year of life, are better equipped to develop appropriate bone size and formation. Maintaining an ideal weight and exercising regularly throughout all stages of life will also reduce the risk.

Diet Changes

One topic to consider as your dog gets older is the need to change to another formula of dog food. If your older dog is less active simply due to age, you might need to provide a lower calorie food made for senior dogs. When you notice some weight changes that could be linked to a mix of excess calories and scaled back activity, talk to your vet about options. You first want to make sure weight changes are due to an underlying condition. When diet changes are in order, do so as needed before your dog gains too many pounds. Obesity and carrying around unnecessary weight can contribute greatly to the development of some very serious health issues.

Heart Disease

Heart disease is another issue that can develop anytime during your dog's life, with a risk that increases with age. Heart conditions are common in all breeds of dogs, with no preference for size or pedigree. Even generally healthy pets can experience a seemingly sudden onset of heart problems.

Myocardial disease is the main type of heart condition seen in large breed dogs, including Labradors. This condition involves a muscle-related malfunction that causes abnormal degrees of dilation and contraction. Simply put, the heart becomes too weak to do its job efficiently, or the muscle becomes too thick to pump sufficiently. While this issue is developing inside, on the outside, there is no clear evidence.

Your dog could be less willing to exercise, have a smaller appetite, and drop a few pounds. All behaviors that could easily pass for typical responses to aging.

Symptoms of Heart Condition

- Lethargy and lack of interest in exercise
- Faltering when standing or walking
- Fainting
- Coughing, wheezing, or hacking
- Shortness of breath
- Drop in agility levels
- Noticeable weight changes

The signs of a heart problem are slight in the first stages of development, and often there are no apparent symptoms until the condition turns life-threatening.

Additionally, the symptoms match a variety of other issues, including those that come with age.

One way to verify heart-related symptoms involves frequent screenings. Talk to your vet about any heart health concerns you have. Simple steps can provide information on heart function, assisting in early detection of developing issues. For example, checking the sound of the heart, the heart rate, and blood pressure can demonstrate normal activities or provide evidence of a problem. If anything signals an abnormality, other tests may be in order. The next step in the screening could involve ultrasounds, x-rays, and ECGs. These procedures can provide early detection of a heart malfunction, allowing intervention before the onset of congestive heart failure.

Steps in Screening for Heart Problems

- Listening for heart murmurs or signs of lung congestion
- Checking pulse rate for unusual palpations
- Taking x-rays to check the size of the heart
- Using EKG to check for enlargement or irregular beats

If congestive heart failure has developed, however, there are treatment options, and a variety of medications to help improve functioning. You can work with your vet to find a suitable plan.

Lastly, if heartworm prevention has not been routine, the infection could result in serious heart issues. Blood tests can verify or rule out this possibility.

Diabetes

Diabetes is another condition that has a higher chance of developing as dogs age.

The disease is a dysfunction related to the body's ability to properly convert nutrients into energy needed for a variety of essential internal functions. The condition involves a deficiency in glucose usage insulin levels. Glucose is commonly called blood sugar and it provides energy for organ and cell functions. Insulin is a hormone that delivers glucose to where it is needed.

When there is a deficiency with the function of this partnership, the result is diabetes. There are several technical terms used to define the root of the dysfunction, but the end result is the same-the body doesn't have the necessary fuel.

To make up for this lack, other sources of energy come from sources of fat and protein that the body breaks down to compensate.

Matters complicate further as sugar levels in the blood increase to a poisonous level. The poison then damages the eyes, heart, nervous systems, and kidneys.

Watch for Symptoms

As with all serious conditions, the sooner you know, the better the odds of successful intervention.

The early signs, again, are similar to other conditions, but one symptom specific to diabetes is unquenchable thirst. If your dog chronically drinks excessive amounts of water and still seems to want more, this is a telltale sign of a blood sugar issue. Keep in mind, there will be times when your dog finishes off entire bowls of water, whether it's due to heat or the activity of the day. Thirst as a symptom of diabetes is not just a one-time deal. It's ongoing.

Along with thirst, the appetite would increase as well. Your dog's chronic hunger is due to signals from the body that nutrient levels are insufficient. Ironically, though, your dog could lose weight, as nutrients pass through the body, unused.

Also going hand in hand with the first symptom, as you can imagine, there would be an increase in urination. Your dog would require many more trips outside or could begin to have accidents inside as well. If you remember from the kennel training section, dogs don't like to soil the space where they sleep. If diabetes is an issue, however, you could find urine-soaked bedding quite often.

This is an unavoidable consequence of a serious condition, so any type of punishment for indoor accidents would only prove cruel and futile. When such atypical behavior occurs, it's time to contact the vet.

As diabetes progressive, more obvious signs of the health issue arise. The dog would start to turn down food. They could regurgitate often. Their energy level would drop dramatically. And their spirits could spiral downward as well.

Symptoms of Diabetes

- Unquenchable thirst
- Frequent urination
- Loss of bladder control

- Weight changes
- Lethargy

As soon as you notice signs that could relate to diabetes, take your dog in for testing. Blood can be tested for high glucose levels or imbalances with electrolytes in the liver.

When a diagnosis is confirmed in the early stages, the damage to affected organs can be kept to a minimum.

There is no cure for diabetes, but treatment, such as daily insulin injections, are typically inexpensive and can keep levels under control. Consistent timing of the shots from day to day can be somewhat challenging for busy schedules but is essential to maintaining proper functions.

The amount and schedule of insulin or other appropriate control options are topics to discuss with your vet.

The comprehensive plan to manage diabetes is typically multifaceted. The mix most likely entails medicinal intervention, moderate and consistent exercise, precise diet management, and checking glucose levels at least daily.

Even with such a plan in place, you would still need to watch for signs that the condition is not fully being controlled.

Thyroid Issues

The thyroid gland, located in the lower region of the neck, produces hormones specific to maintaining proper metabolism. Any excess or deficiency can wreak havoc on your dog's health.

When the thyroid fails to produce the normal volume of hormones, the condition is called hypothyroidism. Large to medium-sized breeds have a higher incidence of this disorder than smaller breeds. The insufficiency results in a sluggish metabolism. The lack also has a negative effect on some organs.

Symptoms of the condition include disinterest in exercise, inattentiveness, increase in weight without diet changes, inability to tolerate cold, and hair loss. As with anything that causes concern, visit your vet to have your dog evaluated. Hypothyroidism has various causes but can usually be controlled with medication. Hyperthyroidism is not often found in dogs.

Obesity can creep up at any age, and excess weight puts your dog at risk for most of the diseases mentioned previously. If getting weight under control becomes challenging, consult your vet for advice.

Incontinence

Incontinence is typically an issue that can occur in middle age to senior female dogs. The first sign of this issue is some leakage of urine, both during activity and inactivity. As the problem develops, you could notice increasing amounts of dampness in bedding.

The problem can have a number of root causes, from urinary tract infections to a weakened bladder.

Don't assume the issue is merely age-related and untreatable. In some cases, there are treatments and medications that can improve the condition.

Eyes

In addition to health concern with involving

internal functions, Labs can also have conditions that affect the eyes. Some can occur at any age while others are more specific to age-related complications.

The cornea is the surface of the eye that consists of thin material similar to skin. This area, like any other surface, can be damaged and injured. Corneal scratches are quite common for dogs like Labradors that like to run top speed though outdoor areas with eyes with and tongue out. This activity can result in surface damage to the cornea if contact occurs with low branches, thick vegetation, or other natural sharp-edged items. Surface scratches pose no long-lasting damage or problems, but they can be very painful nonetheless. There is not much that can be done resolve the damage, other than prescription eye drops that help soothe the cut while it heals. Fortunately, the cornea recovers quickly and your dog will soon be romping again through the woods.

Corneal ulcers rarely do much speed healing. There is also a contribution condition called **dry eye** that can lead to the frequent occurrence of ulcers. The technical term for this condition is keratoconjunctivitis sicca or KCS, and it involves a dysfunction of the tears duct. Sometimes the ducts fail to produce a sufficient level of tears to protect the eyes by clearing away particles and keeping the corneal surface moist. The treatment depends on the severity of the condition. For mild cases of KCS, the vet can provide moisturizing eye drops that need to be applied frequently and on a daily basis. Severe cases sometimes require surgical intervention to correct the problem.

End-of-Life Considerations

With all the challenges you've overcome while raising your puppy, training your dog, then caring for your senior citizen, none take near the courage you'll need to say goodbye.

In the perfect scenario, your dog grows old gracefully and passes peacefully while sleeping. That does happen, but not always.

Some very painful conditions are incurable, and your dog could suffer greatly toward the end of life. It's difficult to know when it's time to let go. You don't want your dog to suffer. You don't want to end his life too soon. Vets often say, "You'll know when it's time." You won't know absolutely.

There are some questions to ponder that can give you perspective. Then you can decide knowing your best friend's interests in mind.

Some issues to first consider involve abilities.

- Can your dog stand on his own?

- Can he enjoy any type of interaction?

- Is he able to eat and drink readily?

- Does your dog react to his all-time favorites?

- Will your dog accept favorite treats?

- Is your dog interested in a favorite toy?

- Does your dog seem open to his favorite show of affection (for instance, tummy rubs, neck massages, scratching behind the ears)?

One tool that might be helpful when gauging your dog's current quality of life is a scale you can find using this link: https://journeyspet.com/pet-quality-of-life-scale-calculator/

Comfort

Reduce pain and provide as much comfort possible when your elderly pet is suffering from a condition that can't be improved further. Some items to consider involve bedding and blankets.

You should consider providing a soft surface when bone and joint pain are present. Beds made specifically for dogs are available in a variety of styles to suit particular needs. You can always consult your vet for ideas on proper bedding and other orthopedic devices and could improve pain levels. Frisco ortho beds and Fur Haven orthopedic sofa are two options for providing extra cushion for areas of pain.

Blankets should be supplied readily, both for comfort and warmth. Elderly pets with terminal illness often have increased sensitively to cold. They should be provided with sufficient coverings, and often several that can be layered. You want your dog to be able to rearrange the blankets as needed. Their ability to nudge heavy blankets aside could be waning so make only thinner layer of blankets actually cover the body.

You can place soft heavy blankets around your pet to offer the feeling of support and safety. This can also aid in keeping particularly painful areas of the floor if that is an issue of concern. The thicker blanket can be used as a type of wedge in one area that serves to lessen the pressure the painful area receives when full weight rests directly on the painful region.

Even if your dog no longer displays interest in its favorite things, that doesn't mean the items no longer have appeal. In pain and weakness, your dog might not be able to show recognition or positive emotions, even when the feelings are present.

Place special items close to your dog, and the sight of them could bring some peace. Remember your dog's most favorite thing is you. Remain present as much as you can during this time. Some diseases can cause health to deteriorate rapidly, and you'll need to continually monitor the situation.

Checklist for Elderly Dog

- Keep bedding soft with plenty of cushions
- Use layers of lightweight blankets
- Place heavy blankets beside and around your dog
- Surround your dog with favorite toys
- Be present to provide companionship
- Closely monitor health conditions
- Look for signs that end-of-life decisions could be in order

Also, dogs can reach a point where they can no

longer control their bowels and bladder. When this is a possible scenario for your dog, be sure to check the bedding often. Change any wet or soiled bedding immediately to avoid infection, especially if your dog develops sores of any kind.

If your dog is well enough to go outside to use the bathroom but has trouble walking alone, you can use a towel as a sling. Make sure the towel is large enough to place under your dog, near and toward the backside, and you have enough left on either side to hold onto. This towel acts like a sling to aid and support your upright dog. Make sure you have enough length of both ends of the towel to grip tightly.

Even with all the care and concern you have for your elderly dog, you could reach a point where the suffering becomes too extreme. As mentioned previously, gauge the quality of life your dog now has versus pain and suffering levels to decide if euthanasia would be the humane choice.

End-of-Life Decisions

Euthanasia involves an injection that acts quickly and painlessly. It can be a peaceful end to a dog's suffering. Often your vet will suggest a sedative to be administered first, but this is a matter of choice. Sometimes the sedative helps calm the dog so administering the next injection won't be a struggle. The dog then passes in quickly, in an average of ten seconds. You will be given the choice to remain in the room throughout the procedure or to stand outside the exam room until after your dog has passed.

The vet will allow you to spend time alone with the dog momentarily after the process is over. Depending on the plans you have for putting your dog to rest, the vet will proceed accordingly.

Most likely, someone in the office will place your pet in an appropriately sized box for transport. If you have a special box or receptacle you would prefer over something made from cardboard, that is an option. You would want to have this item prepared in advance and possibly already in your vehicle in the event that health conditions change suddenly and rapidly.

Cremation and Burial

Traditionally, dogs are put to rest in the yard of their home, under an old oak tree, with some type of homemade memorial marker. Cremation is another option that has become another common option at the end of life.

You will have a choice between individual cremation or as part of a group cremation. The first option will allow you to keep the ashes as a memorial of your dog if that is desired. The second option typically results in the combined ashes being spread over a garden made for this particular purpose or a similar meaningful outdoor location.

A third option involves purchasing a plot in a pet cemetery if the service is provided in your area.

Summary

The experience of having a Labrador retriever in your life is often full of fun times and opportunities to make memories that last a lifetime. Ownership, however, requires the commitment of both time and money. Labradors are very social, as you have learned, so require a lot of time, attention, and patience.

Patience is especially needed during puppyhood when your pet will be learning proper behavior. Training at that point won't happen overnight, and you could lose a couple pairs of slippers before your puppy outgrows the chewing stage.

In the first year, your dog will require training, both for social manners and obedience. Luckily, Labs have a reputation for being highly intelligent and responsive to training. Once Labs reach adulthood, they typically make up for their puppy antics. Full-grown Labs can suit many types of lifestyles, as long as there is ample time for exercise and sport. Labs have a fun-loving disposition but, at the same time, tend to be mild-mannered.

These attributes have made the breed the top dog for families in America, popularity-wise. They are also a top choice for many hunters who are looking for a loyal companion as well as a reliable sporting assistant. Their multi-faceted abilities mixed with the lion's share of personality add up to a four-legged friend who aims to please.

Remember, though, Labradors require room to run and daily opportunities to do so. You need to have enough time to devote to activities utilize their high energy constructively.

Labs can also have their share of health conditions, both specific to breed through heredity and due to their size and weight. To avoid these difficulties, make sure to use the tips for finding the right breeder and the ideal puppy that was addressed in the first chapter. Proper breeding is essential for ensuring a puppy will grow into a well-balanced adult, both mentally and physically. Of course, there are exceptions to every rule, but most breeders offer some degree of guarantee.

Financial investments are definitely one big commitment that comes with ownership. As mentioned in previous chapters, quality food, preventative care, and any unexpected medical conditions can become quite costly. There are a few payment options for medical and programs to help with spaying and neutering costs. For the other responsibilities of ownership, the rule to remember is "buy the best you can afford."

Conclusion

With all the advice of experts and trainers and veterinarians and breeders, the decision on whether or not to bring a Lab into your home ultimately boils down to one question: What's in it for me?

For Melissa Phillips, avid Lab lover and author of *Lessons from Ruthie Jane*, the answer is a million extra moments to treasure. Her dog Ruthie remains a member of the family and has been a companion for her sons throughout childhood. Melissa said she has learned a lot about life by seeing the world through the eyes of a Labrador retriever, some more valuable than those learned through her own experiences.

She says her dog wakes up every day, expecting a good time, and she manages to find something to enjoy, regardless of the situation or level of health. This approach to life is something to cultivate, and life with a Lab can contribute successfully to helping reach that goal.

The lively, friendly demeanor doesn't always prove appropriate, however.

"I guess you could say the biggest challenge and the best thing about owning Ruthie are one and the same," Melissa says. "She has very high energy, and she is quite the social butterfly. She has never met a person she didn't like. Taking her out for walks in a public place can sometimes be awkward when she comes across someone who doesn't care for dogs—especially high-energy dogs. However, that people-loving energy she has is the best thing about owning her because she doesn't like to be outside alone. She needs me to go with her on walks and trips to the park, so she is the reason I get out and get some exercise. I'm pretty sure she has been good for my health."

Many people expect to teach their dogs about the world. Rarely do they realize, before owning a Lab, just how much they can learn from their dog. But if they pay attention, the dog can bring much wisdom to their lives, about life, love, and endurance. It's a win-win for all parties involved. Most often the dog teaches the biggest life lessons of all. Owners learn about the rewards that come from patience; they see an honest display of unconditional loyalty, they learn the benefit of maintaining health through lifelong effort, and they finally understand the strength required when it's time for a final farewell. Such lessons aren't learned through observations. They come from the expeditions you'll take when you have a Labrador at your side.

Book 2:
The Labrador Retriever Training Handbook

The Essential Guide To Potty Training Your Puppy, Teaching Commands, Dog Socialization, And Curbing Bad Behavior

Introduction

Dogs are man's best friend. For thousands of years, dogs have acted as a companion, a team member, and a comforting friend to people all over the planet. Having a dog in your life can be the difference between a home that is empty, quiet, and lonely and having a home that is vibrant, warm, and loving. Dogs serve as a faithful companion that is always loving and accepting, no matter who you are or what you do.

It is widely believed that dogs were the first animals humans domesticated, going all the way back to the hunter-gatherer days where wolves and humans worked together to find and catch food. Wolves, with their spectacular sense of smell and hearing, would lead humans to the animals they would consider to be prey. Wolves were very good at finding these types of prey animals, but not so good at taking them down. This is where humans, with primitive tools such as bows and arrows and spears, would step in to make the kill. This relationship appeared out of necessity and probably took place independently across hundreds of different groups of people across the world. It isn't known when exactly this practice began, but it likely continued for thousands of years until dogs developed a great trust in humans. Simply put, the dogs more inclined to trust and live in close proximity to humans had a better chance at surviving than the dogs that treated humans with suspicion or hostility.

It is widely known that dogs evolved from some kind of wolf, though all species of wolves that we know today (gray wolves, Indian wolfs) appear to be close enough genetic relatives of the dog to be the species they evolved from. As a result, most researchers believe that the species dogs evolved from is now extinct.

Somewhere along the way during this primitive relationship, humans invented agriculture and more and more of them began to live their lives in one place. As this happened, dogs went from friends on the trail to friends in the home. They became more and more widespread and integrated into the home-centered lifestyle. Somewhere along the line, humans figured out the process of selective breeding and began choosing which dogs to breed together to bring out certain traits that they desired. Over centuries, this led us to develop thousands of different breeds of dogs we see today.

But this book isn't just about any dog. This book is about a breed of dog of which few other types of breeds are more popular, beloved, or instantly recognizable. I am speaking of course about the Labrador Retriever. Labrador Retrievers are a type of retriever gun-dog. Retrievers are the type of dogs that help hunters by retrieving the prey they kill. Gun-dogs are types of dogs that help hunters both find and retrieve prey, which usually comes in the form of birds or other small game. Labrador Retrievers are very desirable dogs for almost any dog owner. They're friendly, adaptable to most types of lifestyles, and intelligent.

Of course, developing a good relationship with your Labrador Retriever can require more than giving it a home with plenty of space, exercise, and food. Having a well-trained dog has many advantages for both you and your pup.

The first reason having a well-trained dog can improve both your and your dog's life is that the basic nature of the process of training will give the two of you a great bond. Part of the requirements of training is that you and your dog must spend a great amount of time together. This has a few obvious benefits. First, it gives you the chance to really get to know your dog, what they like, what they don't like, and things that may trigger undesirable behavior. Second, it gives your dog a chance to really feel important and valued because of the fact that the two of you are spending so much time together.

The second reason that the process of training your dog can have a positive effect on both of you is the fact that it will inevitably strengthen the bond between both of you. At the same time, as your pup will have an easier time sensing and reacting to your mood, you will also have an easier time sensing and reacting to your pup's mood and actions.

The third benefit of training your Labrador Retriever is that it's fun. Just playing with your dog might get boring at a point, but the process of training is different. As you put in the time to train your dog, you will have the enormous pleasure of watching the fruits of your efforts. As your dog learns to execute the basic commands we'll cover in this text, you get to watch your dog go from a scatter-brained little pup to a full-grown, disciplined dog that gives off distinct vibes of intelligence and understanding.

The next benefit of training your Labrador Retriever is that the process of training often makes undesirable behavior disappear completely from your dog. Most people know someone or have experienced themselves the embarrassment of having an untrained dog displaying just how untrained it is when meeting someone new, either by jumping on them, barking or through some other undesirable behavior. By training, you substantially eliminate the chances of your dog being viewed as undisciplined. It also makes things easier for you in the long run, letting you exercise more control over your dog by expending far less effort.

The next benefit is that the process of training has numerous and enormous benefits for your pup. Learning how to respond to and execute commands gives your dog a sense of purpose in their lives. It makes them feel valued and fulfilled. At the same time, it stimulates your dog's mind and serves as a platform for mental development.

The next benefit is that it improves your dog's life. Dogs that are well-trained are far less likely to be given up or returned to the shelter. They're also far less likely to have to be put down to behavioral issues. Also, the process of training can turn anti-social, shy, or generally fearful dogs into dogs with a healthy amount of confidence and friendliness.

In this book, we're going to cover a lot of topics. We'll discuss what you should know about Labrador Retrievers before you commit as well as things you can do to prepare your home for your new friend. Then we'll go into the different places you can get a Labrador Retriever. I'll give you some suggestions on what to do before you start training as well as the right ages to start prepping your dog for training. Most of the book will be spent describing the different types of strategies for teaching your Labrador Retriever to do basic commands, potty-training, fetching, and how to behave on a leash. We'll also discuss how to understand and learn from your dog's behavior.

What to Know Before You Commit to a Labrador Retriever

C hoosing to get a dog is a potentially decades-long commitment. Like any long-term commitment, you should first make sure you have the resources you need in order to give your new friend a good, loving home. This section will cover everything you need to know in order to set yourself up for a successful relationship with your dog.

What Is a Labrador Retriever?

Labradors are one of the most popular breeds of dogs. They are often trained to be disability assistance dogs for people who are blind, autistic, or have other physical disabilities. They're also often trained to be therapy dogs.

Labrador Retrievers are descendants of the Saint John's Water Dog, which were mainly in England and Newfoundland, Canada. Their ancestors date back to the mid-eighteen hundreds and were a distinct breed of dogs by the 1870s. Their name comes from two places. First, the name "retriever" was given to them because they were often used as hunting dogs and retrieved birds and other small game.

Second, the name "Labrador" comes from the place where they first originated; the Labrador Sea, which lies between the Labrador Peninsula and Greenland off the east coast of Newfoundland.

Labrador Retrievers has a distinct appearance. Their heads are wide with a flat stop at their nose. Their coat is short and dense and has a color dependent on their sub-breed; either yellow, black, or brown. Their body typically is a stout build and is fairly muscular. The Labrador Retriever's size can vary based on whether it is a male or female. Males usually weigh between 65 to 80 pounds while females usually weigh between 55 to 70 pounds.

One thing that sets Labrador Retrievers apart is their temperament. Most Labrador Retrievers are friendly, out-going, and pleasant. They're much less prone to aggression than other dogs of their size, which makes them very good family dogs. This also makes them good for households with other animals which can be either bigger or smaller than themselves. They're also very good around children as it is not easy to make them act aggressively, given that it has been raised in a healthy environment. Labrador Retrievers may bark occasionally, but most of the time they're not overly-noisy, making them very suitable for urban or suburban environments. They're also not usually very territorial, making them excellent pets when in the proximity of other dogs.

Another thing that sets Labrador Retrievers apart from other dogs is their intelligence. This, combined with their friendliness and calm nature, making them very suitable for positions as working dogs. They are used for a variety of purposes. As previously stated, they're often used as disability assistance dogs. But they're also used for a variety of other purposes. They're often used by bird-hunters to retrieve game. They're also capable of emergency assistance in people prone to seizures and other fits of unconsciousness.

The Types of Labrador Retrievers

There are two main, distinct types of Labrador Retrievers: Yellow Labrador Retrievers and Chocolate Labrador Retrievers. They came about through a few dog breeders who wanted a type of dog that was cool-headed and would bring the game back unharmed to hunters. Today, most Labrador Retrievers live out their lives as simple pets for families.

The Yellow Labrador Retrievers we know today, like almost all dogs, were much different than the dogs they descended from. Back in the mid-nineteenth century, the "yellow" Labrador Retrievers were still yellow but were a much darker shade than the ones we know today. In fact, their coats were what we would call butterscotch, much darker than what we know today. For a while, these types of dogs were called Golden Retrievers, but this was changed by the UK Kennel Club on the grounds that "golden" was not a color. This type of Labrador Retriever went through a slow but consistent change in their appearance over the course of the 20th century as it was common for people to desire lighter-colored yellow dogs over the dirty-looking yellow dogs. As a result, more and more breeders centered on making their pups more cream colored in order to sell more dogs. Over the course of decades, this practice gave way to the light-colored Yellow Golden Retrievers we know today.

Chocolate Labs were not considered a distinct breed until about half-way through the 20th century. While some researches have traced modern Chocolate Labrador Retrievers to a few original bloodlines, some believe their appearance to be the result of cross-breeding, specifically with the Flat-Coated Retriever as well as the Chesapeake Bay Retriever. This was mostly done during the 20th century in Newfoundland. By the second half of the 20th century, Chocolate Labrador Retrievers were known as a distinct breed in the kennels of the Earl of Feversham.

Besides dividing the types of Labrador Retrievers by their color types, there's also a division to be made by origin as well as purpose. These two types are the English Labrador and the American Labrador. The English Labrador is more often used for dog shows and other such types of competitions. The American Labrador is more often used as a working dog and as a family pet.

The American Labrador is usually sharper and more physically fit than its English counterpart. It's also largely more reactive than English Labradors. This isn't to say that they are more prone to bad behavior, just that they're more sensitive to their surroundings. As a whole, they still have a good temperament compared to other dog breeds. They also have more energy than English Labradors. This is because they're more often been bred as working dogs as well as hunting dogs. This means that your Labrador Retriever will require a good amount of activity and exercise to keep it happy.

English Labrador Retrievers often weigh more than their American Labrador Retriever counterparts. They also typically have shorter, stouter arms and legs. While they are active with a lot of energy when they are young dogs, most

American Labrador Retrievers grow into more active adult dogs than English Labrador Retrievers who tend to become calmer and less active when they get older. As puppies, they're also often harder to train than American Labrador Retrievers because they are more scatterbrained on average. They like to play and might get distracted more easily.

There are subtle differences between the different types of Labrador Retrievers, but these differences shouldn't necessarily dissuade you from getting a certain one. They are, as a breed, largely friendly, easy to control, and wonderful companions.

Is a Labrador Retriever Right for You?

There are several things to consider before you commit to a Labrador Retriever. One concern many people have when considering getting a large dog as active as a Labrador Retriever is whether or not they have enough space to keep their dog happy, though this isn't as big of a concern as you might think. Having a huge amount of space for your Labrador Retriever to stomp around on doesn't mean much if you aren't consistently spending time with it. They're not going to be active (or happy) if they're left alone by themselves day after day. What's really important to consider is whether you have enough time to spend with it during the day. Just going for an hour long walk every day is probably sufficient to keep your Labrador Retriever healthy and happy.

Another thing to consider is whether or not your home itself is big enough to keep a Labrador Retriever happy. For example, if you're living in a small apartment and will be gone for a majority of the day, you shouldn't get a dog that requires the kind of space and activity that a Labrador Retriever does. They also like to be involved in things. If you're looking for a dog that likes to sit on the couch and watch you go about your day, a Labrador Retriever isn't for you. They like to play and be involved in most of what they see going on.

Another thing to consider before getting a Labrador Retriever is whether or not you have the funds to take proper care of a Labrador Retriever. The costs can be more expensive than you might think. Expenses like vaccinations are obvious medical costs, but should your dog get sick or get injured in some way, vet bills can get into the thousands. If you have a dog that's in an environment that might make it prone to injury (like a rural area with wild animals or farm animals). This is a possibility that happens to many pet owners. A smart thing you can do to prepare yourself for this by protecting yourself financially and making sure your pet can get the care it needs is to get pet insurance. This is usually paid monthly and can stack up over time, but it is worth it to have a plan to pay for vet expenses should your dog have some medical issue that requires expensive operations. Labradors also have many diseases they can inherit.

Besides vet expenses, there's also the cost of food and grooming tools to think about. You also might want to consider the costs of getting a chip put in your dog should they get lost. That way, you'll have a way of easily finding them.

Another thing you should consider before getting

a Labrador Retriever is the amount of clean-up you'll have to do for your dog. Unlike us, dogs do not have the desire to keep themselves or their environments clean. They like to roll around in the mud and get dirty. They have no problem getting wet. If your dog is going to be going outside and inside a lot, it's inevitable they're going to get dirty at least a few times. This can mean them tracking mud into your house as well as stinking up the place with that "wet-dog smell." If you're very afraid of germs and can't stand getting your hands or your house dirty (even if it can be easily cleaned up), you might want to consider that before getting a Labrador Retriever.

Why Are Labrador Retrievers so Popular?

The Labrador Retrievers are the most popular dog breeds in the United States, and there are many reasons for that.

First, Labrador Retrievers are highly intelligent. There's a reason they are so often used as service dogs. They are fast learners and quick to pick up on new commands. Not only does this make them easy to control, but it also makes them very compatible with jobs and tasks many other dogs couldn't do. They like challenges and doing new things, making them good pets for people that are adventurous and would like to have a dog that's easily handled.

Labrador Retrievers are also popular because they are very gentle dogs who are not prone to aggression. Certain breeds of dogs are very territorial or defensive of their home turf or food (there's actually a test to measure how aggressive a dog is by sticking a fake hand into a food dish while the dog is eating). These types of problems are not often found in Labrador Retrievers. This means that they are a good choice for people in environments that are more social or chaotic than usual, as Labrador Retrievers are good at adapting non-aggressively to these types of environments. As a result, Labrador Retrievers are a good choice for people who have households with other dogs or small children. Labrador Retrievers are actually well-known for the gentleness they show when they're around children. Like all puppies, Labradors can bite and nip from time to time when they're young. But this habit is much easier to train out of them than it is in most other dog breeds. They can learn how to be gentle without sacrificing the joy you'll get with playing with them. Besides getting along very easily with other dogs, Labs love company in the form of all kinds of animals including cats, goats, ferrets, and any other type of furry pet you might have in or around your home.

While Labrador Retrievers do have certain inherited diseases they are at risk for (which is true for almost every type of dog breed), they have, on average, fewer health problems than other breeds of dogs. This gives a number of different benefits for the owner. First, it relieves the stress that comes with owning a dog that has habitual health problems. Second, it means the owners of Labrador Retrievers will not have the same kind of financial strain due to vet expenses that some other owners of different breeds of dogs often face. Third, it means that your Labrador Retriever will be a part of your family for a long time. Labradors live long, active lives; still loving exercise, games, and activity well past when they turn a decade old.

Another benefit of owning a Labrador Retriever is the fact that they're easier to groom than other breeds that shed more often or have longer, thicker, and messier coats. This saves you trips to the groomer as well as the dreaded dog hair all around your house and furniture.

Labrador Retrievers also are good helpers. They love to be involved and are always excited to have "jobs" or certain purposes they can help you with. They love to tag along while playing sports and are quite competitive with other dogs when playing their own games. You'll never have a problem getting your Lab off the couch.

Labs also have very versatile diets. They don't need high-end pet food (though it helps) to stay healthy, active, and full of energy. Dogs can eat almost anything, and Labs are no exception. Another aspect of Labs that people might not immediately think as being a benefit is that there is plenty of them available. Being the most popular dog breed in the United States means that it's a pretty safe bet that you can find breeders of Labs in your area as well as at almost any pound or human society.

Getting a Labrador Retriever

There are many easy ways to get a Labrador Retriever. Based on how much you're willing to spend, what age of Lab you want, and whether having a pure-bred Labrador Retriever matters to you, there are certain things you should know about the different places to adopt or buy a Labrador Retriever before you make the commitment. In this section, we'll cover some of the most common places people find their new best friends.

Types of Dog Breeders

Not all dog breeders are created equal. While most of them can offer the same thing (pure-bred dogs or desirable mixes), knowing what to look for in the different places that breed dogs is important for two main reasons. First, it can mean the difference between getting a healthy dog and a sick dog. Second, it can stop you from supporting cruel businesses that breed their dogs in inhumane ways such as "puppy mills." These places raise dogs, cats, and other domesticated animals in environments that are often dirty, unsanitary, crowded, cruel, and generally do not provide a good place for these animals to live.

If you're looking to get a dog from a breeder, you should know how to find and identify what is called a *Responsible Breeder*. Before we discuss what makes a responsible breeder, we'll start by discussing the places you should always avoid. You are probably familiar with at least a few types of retail chain pet-stores such as Petco, PetSmart, Petland, Pet Supplies Plus, and many other retail chain pet-stores. While we can't say that every animal these stores sell come from puppy mills or other such places, we can safely say that they have been known to get their animals from breeders that would be considered puppy mills. At any one of these locations, you can't know what kind of environment these animals come from. By buying animals from these places, you are inadvertently supporting these kinds of inhumane breeders.

Now we'll talk about how to find a Responsible Breeder. Breeders can range from a small operation done only part-time, to a huge farm that has hundreds of different dogs. But no matter what the size, there are a few things you can do to ensure that you're getting your dog from a humane place.

First, you should the breeder is knowledgeable about the dogs they're raising and kind to them. Second, you should ask to visit the environment where the dogs are raised in and also to see the parents of the dog you're interested in buying. This can give you an idea of what the dog's behavior will be when they are grown. Third, you should take a good, long look at the kennels or general property. You should look to make sure the area is clean, that the dogs have plenty of space and food, and for any signs of bad health such as sores, patches of bare skin, and other such signs. Lastly, make sure the breeders are open and honest about any problems they've encountered with their dogs. They should not seem secretive or put off by questions you have every right to ask.

One benefit of getting you Lab from breeders is that you can usually get them as puppies, making them easier to train and more easily integrated into your home. By buying from breeders, you have the opportunity to see both the parents of the dogs as well as the environment in which they were raised. It is also easier to get Labs that are purely labs, or at least Labs for which you know exactly what it is mixed with if it is a mix.

A few disadvantages of getting your Lab from breeders is that it can sometimes be hard to find a good breeder if you live in a sparsely populated area. They are also probably the most expensive place to get your Lab compared to pounds or humane societies, which we will talk about next.

Shelters, Rescues, and Pounds

Shelters, rescues, and pounds are often used interchangeably, but they are quite different from each other. A majority of the dogs that end up in these places aren't there because they're bad dogs or did anything wrong. Usually, dogs end up in these places because their previous owners had to give them up due to circumstances outside of their control. So don't be scared. All of these places are filled with friendly dogs that will make wonderful pets!

Rescues accept dogs that shelter or pound either couldn't or wouldn't take. This can be because of a few reasons. First, shelters and pounds, especially in large cities, are prone to overcrowding and often simply don't have space for some certain unfortunate dogs. They also might not take dogs because of aggressive or other types of undesirable behavior, usually stemming from abuse. Rescues, which are usually non-profit organizations operated by volunteers, take these dogs in and often focus on rehabilitation and placement. One benefit of getting a dog from rescues is that the staff there will usually have a good idea of the dog's needs, temperament, and other personality traits which can help you decide whether or not the dog is a good fit for your home.

Probably the best-known animal shelter in the United States is the Humane Society. They are privately owned charities. Shelters can be as small as having a few dogs looking for a home to as big as having hundreds of dogs on its property. Some are even as big as to have full on marketing teams that hold events for adoption or for fundraising. Like rescues, these organizations can give you a good idea of the behavior of any certain dog before you take it home. But they can be pretty busy, so it may be up to you to follow up on a potential pet. Shelters, unlike rescues, which almost never euthanize animals, could be 'kill shelters' or 'no-kill shelters'. Kill shelters usually keep the dog for a while if they think it's a good candidate for adoption. But, depending on the amount of space available and the number of dogs coming in, they might end up having to put certain dogs down. So if you get your dog from a shelter, you might be saving a life.

Pounds are the saddest type of place you can get a dog from. Unlike shelters or rescues, they don't have much of a focus on saving the lives of animals. The dogs in pounds are usually strays who have been found or pets who have been given up by their owner. If the dog is a stray, the pound gives them a certain amount of time for their owner to claim them, as is required by law. If their owner doesn't show up to claim them, they can be given a little more time to for someone else to come in to adopt them, either a private citizen or a rescue group. If this doesn't happen quickly enough, the dog is usually put down. If you get a dog from a pound, there's a good chance you're saving its life. Unfortunately, the staff there probably doesn't have the resources to really assess the dog, so it's hard to know what kind of dog you're getting.

Starting Young

Once you've found your new Labrador Retriever, there are some things you should know before you bring it home. And, once you've brought it home, if you wish to train it, there are some things you can do right off the bat to give your dog a head start on its training. In this section, we'll cover how to prepare your home for your new Lab. We'll also talk about what to expect during the first week as well as some simple things you can do to prepare it for training as well as what you should do to directly prepare it for training. Then we'll go over how to start curbing basic behavior. Finally, we'll go over how to teach your dog some basic commands every dog should know.

Preparing Your Home

If you're living with other people, the first thing you should make sure of before you bring a dog into your home is that they are okay and ready to share their home with a new friend. This ensures a smooth transition for yourself as you open your home to a dog. It also makes sure that your dog is given a warm, loving environment when it arrives at your home. Everyone in the home should know the breed of the dog, the age of the dog, and perhaps even an idea of its temperament.

Next, you should get everyone in your home on the same page as to which behaviors you either want or don't want in your dog. Everyone should be consistent in which behaviors the dog should be dissuaded from. For example, if you want to stop your dog from excessive licking or biting, everyone in the home should know that this behavior is not acceptable and they should also know the way you're going to curb the behavior. With everyone in the house reacting the same way to a dog's certain behavior, it will make it much easier and quicker to break the dog of that behavior.

Next, you should make sure you have dished for food and water ready at home. You should also have a kind of dog food that is made specifically for your dog's size, age, and activity level. Next, if you're planning on training your dog, you should have treats ready to go so you can start training immediately. This can be dog biscuits, a piece of lunch meat, cheese, or any other type of treat your dog loves to eat. You should also have a collar and leash ready as well as any other type of dog-related tool you might need.

Next, you should set aside certain areas for your dog. If you don't want your Lab on the couch, make sure they have a comfortable, warm place to sleep and relax instead. This can be in the form of a dog bed or simply in the form of a few old blankets, pillows, or quilts.

You should also make sure that your dog has a place to exercise and go to the bathroom. If you have a backyard, you have three options. If your yard has a fence that your lab won't be able to get out of, you can plan on just letting them roam around the backyard. If your fence needs repairs or fixing, make sure that is done before you bring your Lab home. If you don't have a way to keep your dog in or don't want it roaming freely around your yard for whatever reason, you should have a way to tether it to a certain area, either with a rope or a small chain. Or, if you live in a rural area far enough away from busy roads or neighbors, you can plan on just letting your dog run free around your home. They'll know your house is their home in a very short amount of time, though if they start to roam, you might want to restrict their movement.

If you have a puppy, you'll want to make sure your home is "puppy-proof" by putting things that can be chewed up away or out of reach. Puppies have new teeth coming in. As a result, they live to bite and chew on things. Some of the things you should put away or out of reach are shoes, TV remotes, clothes, socks, paper, stuffed animals, and anything else a puppy could chew on. You can also use a type of spray to coat the legs of furniture and other such things that can't be moved to deter your Lab pup from chewing on them. These types of sprays make the surfaces taste bad and unpleasant to your pup. One thing you definitely want to get your Lab pup is something they can chew on because they need to chew on something. This can be a rope, a bone, or some kind of chew-toy.

The First Week

The first week your dog is home will set the mood and dynamic for your whole relationship.

The first thing you should do is give your Lab pup a name. You should use it as often as you can. Chances are they won't respond right away. Something you can do to speed this process up is to call them by their name and then give them a treat. This will make them associate the sound of their name with the pleasure of getting the treat.

If you repeat this enough, every time you say their name, you'll get their immediate attention.

One thing you should do is restrict your pup's movement, keeping it in your line of sight when possible. If you get a Lab puppy, it's unavoidable that they're going to get into some sort of trouble, either chewing something up, knocking stuff over, or going to the bathroom where they shouldn't. You should, if possible, keep your pup out of rooms with carpet, making clean-up easy should they have an accident. This also keeps them from getting into certain rooms that have things they can damage. You can do this by blocking off certain stairways or hallways or by simply shutting a door.

You also want to get your pup on a routine. It might sound strange, but putting some order into a Lab pup's life can make them better behaved, calmer, and more easily trained. Your Lab pup should wake up and go to bed at the same time every day. It helps them get used to the home and the people in it. You should also try to feed and water them at the same time every day. This will help them regulated their digestive system and will reduce the number of accidents.

You should also give them potty breaks as often as possible. If you're home, try to take them out about once an hour, keeping an eye on them and letting them back in directly after they go to the bathroom. This will make them associate the outside with going to the bathroom much quicker than they would otherwise.

During the first week, you want to keep the vibe calm in the house. Moving homes is a big deal to a Lab pup, and it can cause a certain amount of stress. Of course, everyone in the house will want to see and play with the pup. This is okay, but remember that your Lab pup is still growing and developing, and needs a lot of rest as a result. Make sure your home is as free as it can be from loud noises or general chaos for the first couple weeks your Lab pup is home. Don't push them into doing things they're not comfortable with. As your Lab pup gets more comfortable with its environment, it will explore on its own. This isn't to say that you shouldn't play with your new lab pup. You absolutely should. It keeps them active and serves as a great way to bond with them. It also ensures that they'll be tired when it's time to go to bed. Just to be sure not to be too intense when playing with them.

Another thing you should do during the first week your Lab pup is home is to make sure they have a place to sleep that they are comfortable with. When everything gets dark and quiet in this new, unfamiliar place they find themselves in, chances are they're going to get a little scared. This means they might whine and wake you up during the night. Some things you should do to help them feel more comfortable is to make sure they have a place to sleep that is their own. You may also want to make sure they're not sleeping alone. You can put their bed into your bedroom during the first week to make them feel more comfortable with sleeping by knowing they're close to you.

Preparing Your Labrador Retriever Puppy for Training

Puppies have notoriously short attention spans. It also takes Lab pups a while to get used to and comfortable with their environment. Because of these things, it's not a smart idea to start obedience training right away. Not only will they probably not be receptive to it, but it can also give them the wrong idea of you being too demanding or controlling. It used to be the rule that you shouldn't start obedience training until they're six months old. It still is, to an extent, and we'll talk more about that later. Still, there are some basic games you can play to prepare them to respond to commands while still being fun for them.

A basic game you can do with your Lab puppy requires a few people. At least three people are needed, but it gets really fun once you have five or six. Once you have enough people, give them all a few dog treats and have them all stand or sit in a type of circle with lots of space in between them. Put the Lab pup in the middle of the group and take turns calling its name. When it comes to you when you call its name, give it a treat. This game can help them be responsive and attentive while also making them like everyone a lot more.

Another thing you can do requires at least two people. One person gets the puppies attention while the other person gently holds it in the place. Then the first person goes out of sight and hides somewhere, either inside the house or outside the house. Keep calling the lab pup's name, and reward it with a treat and praise when it finds you. As you guys keep playing this game, you can go further and further away. This game teaches your dog to respond to its name while also giving them the challenge of finding you.

A simple game you can do with your puppy requires just yourself, a leash, some treats, and a place to explore. Go somewhere outside where the Lab pup hasn't been before. Let them stop and go where they want, letting them stop to smell or look around. As the Lab pup does this, they'll occasionally look back at you. So every time they look back at you, praise them and give them a treat. Do this over and over again for a while until they're looking back at you constantly. If they don't look at you right away, say their name and give them a treat when they look back. This prepares them for future leash training and makes them more in tune to yourself.

The last basic game you can play with your dog to prepare it for training is the old game of tug of war. It keeps them active and healthy and will wear them out in a pretty short time, making them quieter when it's time to go to bed later. This game can be used to teach your pup two things; when to pick up the toy and when to let the rope go. Choose a different command for both actions and reward them with a treat when they complete the command.

Basic Training

While it may be a while before you should start teaching your dog basic obedience training such as sitting, laying down, staying, or coming, you can almost immediately start trying to control your Lab pup's behavior. Most of this section will be about the different ways you can curb bad behavior in general (we'll get into how to curb specific bad behaviors later in the book).

One thing we should establish right away is that you should try to train your lab pup without using punishment. While physically reprimanding your dog has the reputation of teaching it that you are the dominant one in the group, today it is widely known that this isn't the best way to curb unwanted behaviors. Physically punishing your dog make them more prone to aggressive behavior because you are yourself displaying aggression and dogs largely pick up their behavior and temperament from their owners. It can turn a Lab pup with a few bad behaviors into a dog that's hostile and prone to biting.

Another thing you shouldn't do when trying to curb your Lab pup's bad behavior is to act aggressively towards it. This includes holding it down, staring at it intensely, and intimidating you Lab pup. Using these kinds of methods may curb bad behavior, but it also teaches your dog to act aggressively in certain situations. And that is something you don't ever want in a dog, especially if it's around small children or other animals.

You also shouldn't raise your voice at your Lab pup. When young dogs get scared, they may bow down to you, but it can lead to resentment that results in aggression in the long run. Young dogs usually pick up their temperament from their owners. So if you're anxious and nervous around them, chances are they're also going to grow up to be anxious and nervous. In the exact same way, if you are loud and angry towards your lab pup, chances are they're going to end up being a loud and angry dog.

Now that we've covered the things you shouldn't do when trying to control your Lad pup's behavior, let's go over what you should to curb your lab pup's behavior. The first thing you can do to accomplish this is very simple: be consistent. If you allow or even reward a bad behavior even once, your Lab pup will have in its mind that it's okay in some sense, even if you discourage it a majority of the time. Switching between allowing a bad behavior and discouraging a bad behavior can also confuse your Lab pup, causing stress and perhaps even resentment.

Also, make sure to only discipline your Lab pup if you can catch them while doing the unwanted behavior. If you discipline your pup for something it did a few hours ago, it's not gonna connect the dots between what it did and what it is being disciplined for, even if you try to show them what they did wrong. Even a span of a few minutes between the bad behavior and the discipline can confuse your Lab pup.

While you never want to yell at or physically punish your dog, that doesn't mean you shouldn't take a hard stand against unwanted behavior. You shouldn't raise your voice, but consistently giving them a strong "no" when they do something wrong accompanied by being put outside or a timeout will make them associate that sound with something they shouldn't do which makes it much easier to curb bad behavior in you Lab pup.

Something you can do that will enforce positive behavior while also winning over your Lab pup's affection is using positive reinforcement. It's important to discipline your pup when they display some kind of bad, unwanted behavior.

But, at the same time, it's also important to reward them for positive behavior. You can reward them with praise, with pets, or with their favorite kind of treat.

A good way you can discipline any young Lab pup is through giving them timeouts. While it isn't as harsh as punishing them physically or yelling at them, placing them into isolation directly after they do something bad can be a great way to curb unwanted behavior. In the same way that little kids get bored during timeouts and hate them, dogs are also not big fans of timeouts. They like to play and lock their attention to something. So timeouts can be a great way of curbing behavior by putting them through something they don't like while not confusing, upsetting, or triggering aggression in them. When you put your dog in timeout, you should have prepared some specific verbal signal that is distinct from all other commands.

Without acting angry or upset, you can then gently lead them to a room or area that's small and has little to no things that can entertain your Lab pup. Separating your dog from other dogs or people is a mildly unpleasant experience, and, if you are consistent in meeting bad behaviors with this discipline tactic, it won't take long for them to associate that behavior with something that is unpleasant. This shouldn't be for too long a period of time. Also, they should have access to food and water to keep them comfortable. If they get hungry or thirsty and don't have access to food or water, it can cause them to panic as well as build resentment towards whoever is depriving them of these things.

Essential Commands

There is no magic age at which you should start training your dog. Every dog is different. If you've been preparing them for training by playing certain games and curbing bad behavior, you can probably start training around four to five months old. If you've been waiting until your dog matures to train them, then six to seven months old are probably a good suggestion as to when to start. Whatever age your dog is, you should make sure they can focus and pay attention to you for a good amount of time, as you can't train a dog to do much when they're not even looking or listening to you. If needed, you can go back to some of the games for puppies we've already described to help train your dog to pay attention to you.

Some of the things you should make sure of before beginning to train your dog these basic commands are that you have plenty of time, are well rested and are in a good mood. Some dogs pick up on training quicker than other dogs, but it's safe to say that training any dog requires a lot of patience. You don't want to get frustrated with your dog while training because they can sense your mood, and being afraid of you while learning these commands will cause them stress both during the process as well as every time you give them the command in the future.

In this section, we'll go over some easy ways to train your Labrador Retriever to do the basic commands. As we've already discussed, Labrador Retrievers are smarter than most other dog breeds, so they'll probably be quicker to pick up on these commands than other dogs would be. That is if they're trained the correct way using the correct methods. The purpose of this section is to teach you how to do that in the most effective way possible.

How to Come

Even if you're not interested in teaching your dog

some of the harder commands, one thing all dogs should be able to do is to come to their owner on command. So here's how to do it.

Take your dog and bring them into your home. Make sure you have plenty of their favorite treats. Choose a quiet room that is as free as possible of distractions. Then sit with your dog right next to you and say their name and "come" until they look at you. When they look at you, give them a treat. This is all they have to do at first. Do this many times until they begin to react to only the word "come."

Once they can do this well, put a treat on the floor beneath them. When they're done eating it, say "come" again. When they look at you, give them a treat. Do this over and over again. Slowly, start dropping the treat further and further away from them until they have to walk over and get it, saying "come" when they're furthest from you and rewarding them with a treat when they come to you. Just say the word "come" as much as you can and only use their name if they're really not responding. Using their name too much can make them ignore it after a while. Try to say the command only once. Saying it too often can result in them not responding to it. If they don't come to you when you say the command, take a step closer to them and repeat until they come to you.

Once your puppy learns how to turn around when he hears the command, begin increasing the distance and changing other aspects of the command. Throw the treat further and further. After a while, you can even begin to take a few steps back or move to a different part of the room while they're going after or eating the treat. Once they can respond to your command without fail no matter how far the distance is between you or what part of the room you're in, you can move to other parts of the house and try to call them from other rooms. As you do this, see if they'll come to you without you throwing a treat while still rewarding them with one.

Once they've mastered this, move outside and practice this command over as long a distance as you can. Slowly, start phasing out rewarding them with treats of any kind except praise, rewarding them with treats only if you have to if they start to drop off.

How to Sit

Having a dog that knows how to sit is one of those things most dogs can or should know how to do. While it may not be the most fun, it is a useful command because it keeps your dog in tune with you and reminds them that you are in control.

There are two main ways through which you can teach your dog how to sit.

The first way we'll discuss is called *capturing*. You start by standing before your Labrador Retriever pup while holding some of their favorite treats in your hand. When you start, he should be in the standing position. You should be making eye-contact with him the entire time you're doing this. If you do this for a long enough, they should eventually sit at some point. When you see them do this, praise them and give them a treat. After they've sat down and you've rewarded them, you should now take a step back and keep moving back until they stand up. Once they stand up, keep waiting while holding eye-contact and wait for them to sit and reward them. Repeat the same process, but say sit when they stand up and keep repeating the command until they do it, and then reward them. Do this same process for as long as it takes until they can sit by hearing just one command.

The next method of teaching your dog to sit is

called *luring*. This method of training requires a more intimate interaction with your dog. First, make sure you have plenty of treats they like. Then find a room or a place that has as few distractions as possible. What you want to do is hold the treat right in front of your Lab pup's nose without letting them bite at it or lick at it. Once your Lab pup is nice and focused on it, slowly lift it up while making sure they're following the motion of the treat. As you do this, you should make their nose follows the treat and begins to point up high enough. Eventually, your Lab pup should sit down in order to lift their nose up higher. When they sit, give the treat to them and give them praise. Repeat this a few times. Once they've gotten the hang of it, leave the treats behind and just use your hand to guide them up to the position of sitting. Keep doing this a few times the same way. Once they get the hang of it, start saying "sit" as you guide them up with your hand. Make sure you say the word "sit" right before you give them the hand signal. Repeat this over and over again while slowly phasing out the hand signal until they sit just from the command.

How to Lay Down

You can teach your Lab pup to lay down in the same kind of way you can teach them to sit. Move them into a quiet room with as few distractions as possible and make sure you bring plenty of their favorite treats. Then stand or sit before them while being silent and not moving. Eventually, your dog will either sit or lie down. When your Lab pup lies down, praise them and give them a treat and praise while saying "lay down" or whatever it is you want the command to be. Then prompt them to stand back up using "stand up" or some other cue. If they don't want to stand up right away, you can prompt them to by holding a treat out of their reach, making them stand up to get it. Then wait for them to lay down again, giving them a treat, praising them, and saying the command as they do so. Slowly, you can start phasing out using the treat and just use hand signals. Once they can obey the hand signals without fail, slowly phase them out and only use the command.

You can also use the technique of luring to teach them how to law down. Hold one of their favorite treats beneath their nose and move it down as they try to eat it until they lay down on the floor. When they're on the floor, give them the treat and praise them while saying "lay down" or some other command. Repeat this for as long as it takes until they can do it quickly and consistently without fail. Once they can do this, slowly start phasing out using the treat and only use your hand while still praising them and repeating the command. Once they can lay down only using your hand motion, slowly start phasing out the hand motion and only use the command.

How to Stay

Having a dog that knows how to stay can mean the difference between having a dog that is wild and uncontrollable to having a dog that's easy to control and won't be hard to get a hold of should they get away from you in public for whatever reason. While it may seem like a simple command like the others we've covered so far, correctly teaching a dog how to stay is a lot harder than you may think. Basically what you're doing is teaching your dog to ignore its surrounding and all outside stimuli except for yourself. This section will give you a few different ways to teach your Lab pup how to stay successfully.

Teaching a Lab pup how to stay is more than getting them to sit still on command. In fact, it has two parts. The first is obeying the command you give that signals them to sit. The second is obeying the command you give them that's meant to tell them that they're free to get up. Before you start teaching your dog how to stay, you should've first taught them how to sit. This is necessary for the training process and they should be able to do it consistently.

Really, the words you use for these two commands can be whatever you want. The meaning they have to your dog will depend on what you train them to associate with it. All it is to them is a sound. Knowing this, you should make sure that these two commands sound very distinctly different. This is also true for every other command you might train your dog to respond to. For the command that prompts them to stay, we'll just use "stay" for the purposes of this section. For the command that tells them they can move freely, we'll use "ok" for this section.

In what may seem backward, you should begin by teaching them the command that tells them they can move freely. First, go to a place where there isn't much sound and is free from distractions. Make sure you have plenty of their favorite treats. To start, stand with your Lab pup on one side of the space you're in, making sure they can be held in place. Next, throw one of their treats to the other side of the space you're in. Instead of keeping them from getting the treat, immediately let them go over and get it. As soon as they start over towards it, say the word you've previously chosen that tells them they're free to move. Repeat this process a good number of times, maybe fifteen to twenty at most. This will teach your Lab pup that the sound you're making means to start walking.

Once your dog knows the sound that tells them

they're free to move, make sure you're facing them, prompt them to sit, and praise them with a treat and release them with the word you've already decided on. Then prompt them to sit and face them again, waiting about five seconds before you repeat the same process. Then wait and praise them again with another treat when you release them with the specific word. Do this again and again. Start adding five seconds to the time you wait between each treat you give them. What you're doing here is rewarding them for staying still. Somewhere along the way, your Lab pup will probably move or get up before you release them. All this means is that you have to go back five seconds and increase the time interval slower.

Once your dog can sit for a good amount of time, start adding distance between the two of you. Give them the prompt to sit and then give them the prompt that means "stay" before moving away from them. Take just one step away at first. Then repeat the same process as above after a few seconds of waiting while slowly increasing the distance. If your Lab pup moves before you give them the prompt, simply repeat the process over while moving a shorter distance away from them than you did before. You should build the distance between the two of you very slowly. This makes it easier for your dog and decreases stress for both of you. Once you've gone the distance, give the release word and let them come over to you, prompting them with a treat if needed (treats should be phased out eventually, however).

At first, you should be taking steps backward, facing them the entire time. As the distance increases and they get better at following your commands, begin turning your back to them while walking only short distances at first. You should make sure they can stay while watching you move away a good distance before you proceed to the next step. Once they can, start giving them the prompt to stay while standing a little further away than before. Then give them the release prompt and let them come over to you. Once they can obey the "stay" command and the "free to go" command at a good distance, throw a treat a few feet away. Once they get to it, tell them to stay, wait, and them prompt them to walk away or come over to you. Keep increasing the distance you can throw the treat with them still obeying you until they can do it at great distance without fail.

Teaching them how to stay is a big process that can take a few hours. You may even want to split the process up over a few days to keep them from getting tired or stressed.

How to Potty-Train Your Labrador Retriever

Teaching your Labrador Retriever where it can and can't go to the bathroom is something you should start doing as early as possible. One of the most common reasons owners give up dogs is because they make these kinds of messes inside the house.

Putting up with a dog who you constantly have to clean up after is a hard thing to do. Unless your dog has been potty-trained before you took it home, there will be accidents. The only thing you can do for these is to prepare. Make sure you have paper towels, anti-septic, gloves, and other cleaning supplies. You should also, if possible, restrict your lab pup's movement to places where they can't leave stains. This means not letting them onto furniture until they're broken-in. It also means putting up barriers around your house to keep you Lab pup out of rooms with carpet floors. If you can, try to restrict their movement to rooms with hardwood floors because these floors are much easier to clean up messes on.

Anyone who has ever had a dog will probably tell you that they know how to break a dog in. One of the most common methods (among Americans at least) of house-training your new Lab pup is to rub their nose in their own urine or feces. In regards to this method, there is one thing I want to make clear: you should never do this. While it may teach your dog now to potty inside of the house in the long run, it's a cruel form of punishment for something they don't know better than to do. Dogs have no instinct that tells them there are places they should go and shouldn't go. Using this method of house-training will only make your dog fear you as well as fearing being inside. This can lead to aggression in certain dogs, ruining your relationship with them.

In this section, I'll cover three different types of ways to house-train your dogs. They all have different purposes and are better suited for different environments. Coming up, I'll define the different types and give you an idea of which types of homes are compatible with which type of house training. Then I'll go through and describe the process of teaching your dog each method. Finally, I'll end this section with some very helpful tips to speed up or maintain your dog's behavior.

Kinds of Housetraining and the Types of Homes They're Suited For

There are three main methods for house-training your dog: crate training, outside training, and paper training. We'll go over them in that order.

Crate Training

The method of Crate Training can turn some people off. If you have empathy for Labs at all, you'd probably expect to feel guilty at the idea of keeping your new friend locked in a cage inside your home. But dogs love crates! They have an instinctual desire to seek out a small, confined, and comfortable place that they can turn into their own space. Chances are that, whether or not you provide your new pup with a crate, they'll find some sort of small space where they can sleep.

There's also a lot of benefits for dog owners when they decide to crate train their dog. Having a comfortable and safe place you can put your dog into comes in handy if your dog is excitable (which most young dogs are) and you're having company over, especially considering that you don't have to worry about them making a mess. It's also nice for those who live in apartments or those who can't put their dogs outside for some reason. Also, if you ever need to take your dog somewhere, such as to the vet or on a trip, then crate training will make sure your Lab is already comfortable with being in a crate for extended periods of time.

The concept of crate training requires that the crate is large enough that the dog can relieve itself inside it while still keeping the space where they sleep/lounge clean. Like us, dogs don't like laying in their own waste, so having a specific corner sectioned off for their bathroom needs will prompt them to go there every time.

Outside Training

The concept of outside training is simple; your new Lab pup does its business outside. Sounds simple, right? Well, you'd be interested to know that outside training is actually the hardest method of house-training to do. In the process of house-training, you're probably going to see more accidents than any other method.

Training your dog to go to the bathroom can fit your needs for a number of reasons. If you have multiple dogs, it ensures that you won't have to clean up too many messes once you get them broken in. Or, if your dog is big, it can stop you from cleaning up after them too.

The best kind of environment for outside potty-training your pup is a house with a yard that's either fenced in or a home in a rural area far away from roads and other houses. But if you don't have this kind of place, that's fine too. Just make sure you're okay with taking your dog outside on a leash multiple times a day.

Also, just because your dog does its business outside doesn't mean you won't have to clean up the mess. If you live in an apartment complex or in a condo, you probably know that many of these places require you to pick up after your dog. So make sure you have access to gloves and bags!

Paper Training

Paper training got its name from dog-owners in

high-rise apartments who, instead of taking their dog down a bunch of floors, simply laid down some newspapers and let their dog do its business on those. Of course, if you want, you can still use newspapers for this purpose, just make sure you put down a bunch of them and be prepared to clean up the floor underneath. For the most part, however, most people using this method opt for special pads that are designed to be absorbent and sanitary.

This method is a good choice for owners who live in high-rise apartments or other heavily urban areas that might make it hard for you to take your dog outside. It's also a good alternative method for Lab-owners that either doesn't want to confine their pup to a crate or simply don't want a crate in their home.

Crate Training

Before you start using the crate as a method of potty training, you should get your dog used to the crate itself. This can be a long process. First, buy a crate that gives your dog plenty of space. If your Lab is a puppy, take into account how big they'll be and how much space they'll need when they're fully grown.

Once you've brought home a properly-sized crate for your lab, fill it with some old pillows or blankets and keep them confined to one side. When your Lab gets to the point of regularly using the crate to do its business, you want to make sure they don't make a mess on their "nest." If you want (it's even probably recommended by most), you can put special pads down to absorb their urine and keep it from spilling over.

Then you want to introduce you Lab to their new crate in the kindest way possible. They should associate the crate with nothing but positive things. Never use the crate as punishment. It will make them reluctant to go in it. Try throwing a few dog treats into the crate. When they go to eat them, shut the door and feed them more treats through the wire. The first couple of weeks, you should move the crate into the room so they have the sense that they're not alone. Chances are they'll probably whine the first few nights. If they do this, simply go over, take them out and see if they need to relieve themselves. Once they do or once they haven't gone for a while, praise them and perhaps give them a treat before putting them back in.

Keep them in the crate any time they're out of your sight to prevent accidents. If your dog's more than six months old, you can leave them in there for about six hours (but not much more). If they're only a few months old, take them out every three hours because dogs that young have trouble holding their bladder.

When you take them out, put them down on a pad directly outside the crate. Wait and keep them there until they do their business, repeating some phrases like "go to the bathroom" to help them associate the command with a green light to go. Do this for a few days and then move the pad into the crate. The next time you take them out, put them directly back in on top of the pad and repeat the command. It may take a while, but they should eventually relieve themselves.

You'll want to supervise them during this as often as possible during the learning the process. Once they can do it without accidents, you can simply switch out pads as often as needed.

This isn't to say that crates should be used all

day. At most, they should only be in the crate when they absolutely have to be, like when you're not home or when you have people over. At night, if you're not comfortable with them sleeping with you, you should keep them in the crate with the door closed for the first few weeks. It won't take long for them to realize that this is where they're supposed to sleep. They should start going into it at night by their own will, without you having to put them in there or shut the door.

Outside Training

Teaching your Lab to do its business outside is more complicated than crate or paper training because it requires both you and your dog to operate on a schedule. It also means that you'll have to keep a close eye over what they eat and when they eat. Hopefully, they'll get to the point where they sit by the door or give you a signal when they need to go out. Here's how to get there.

If you're training a puppy (as most of you probably are), you should start potty training immediately. The first few weeks your dogs are home, try to have someone take them out every hour. Keep an eye on them for about ten minutes. Once they relieve themselves, bring them directly back inside. Keep in mind that dogs usually poop twice in each session, so make sure you give them enough time for the second one.

Your dog will pee much more often than they'll go number two. A helpful thing to know is that dogs usually pee about twenty minutes after they drink water. So try to keep track of both when you water and when they go to their water dish, taking them out about twenty minutes after they drink and waiting about ten minutes for them to go.

Another thing you'll want to do is to be consistent in when you feed them. If you're constantly giving them food throughout the day, then food will constantly be moving through their system, increasing the chances for an accident. Feed and water them the same amount at the same times every day. You should also control the times they have access to food. You can do this by leaving the bowl on the ground for as long as it takes for them to get what they need (probably about fifteen minutes) and then picking it up and putting it somewhere that they can't reach it.

When it comes to restricting their access to their water bowl, they should be able to drink water as they need throughout most of the day. However, taking their access to their water bowl away a little while before bedtime can be a good way of decreasing the risk of nighttime accidents. You can probably take away their water dish about two hours before it's time for them to go to bed. If you do this, you should make sure they have access to their water bowl first thing in the morning.

After they do their business, give them praise and repeat certain phrases they can learn to associate with relieving themselves. Make sure you bring them inside as soon as you can after they complete doing their business. Be sure to reward them right away during the first few weeks, starting out with giving them treats and then simply praising them. You don't want to reward or praise your dog after you bring them inside. Instead, you should give them rewards or praise outside immediately after they do their business.

Accidents will happen. As we have discussed

before, you should never punish your dog by shoving their nose into their waste. As with anything a dog does, they will only understand the connection to what you do in response to it if your response is done directly after they do it. If they go to the bathroom inside (which they almost certainly will at some point), you should only react if you catch them in the act. If you do, simply pick them up, say a phrase that they can learn to associate with something they shouldn't do, and put them either outside or in time out.

You should supervise your dog as much as you possibly can during the first few weeks of training. If they're going to the bathroom inside half the time and outside half the time, it's going to take them much longer to learn to go outside to relieve themselves. Therefore, you should try to react to every single time they go to the bathroom, putting them out if they go inside and not giving them praise, and giving them treats and praise every time they go to the bathroom outside.

Paper Training

Letting your dog do its business inside is sure to put a lot of people off. But if you're living somewhere that makes taking them out more difficult than you'd like to deal with multiple times a day, it's probably something you'll have to do. Despite this, it's actually much easier to teach your new Lab pup to do its business on a pad than it is to get them to do it inside. With the right training and methods, it only takes about a week to get your new Lab pup to be consistently going to the bathroom in the right place.

Before you can start training your new Lab pup to do its business on a pad inside the house, you'll need to choose a product. There are three main types of different product that you can use for this purpose: pads designed to absorb and keep the area beneath it dry and sanitary, fake grass, and litter boxes built for dogs. All of these have their own benefits. *Litter boxes* allow your dog to relieve itself multiple times over several days before you have to do any cleaning up because of the chemicals in the litter that prevent smell. *Fake-grass pads* benefit you if your dog has some prior training that tells it that grass is where they're supposed to relieve themselves. *Pads* are usually cheaper and are easily cleaned up. None is absolutely better than the other, so it's up to you to decide which one is right for your needs.

You should start paper potty-training your new lab pup the day you bring him home. Like we've discussed in the section about outside potty-training, you should start working right away to get your dog on a feeding schedule, giving them food at the same times every day and then taking it away after fifteen minutes.

Then you'll want to choose a location you can use every day. Your dog is more likely to associate the place they're allowed to go to the bathroom with a location that the surface they're standing on while they do it. Because of this, you want to pick a confined area that doesn't see much traffic. The smaller the better. Ideally, the pad, fake-grass, or litter box should take up the entirety of the area you designate to place them.

Like with outside training, this method of housebreaking requires you to keep a very close eye on your dog for the first couple weeks. Pick them up and put them on the pad or litter box or whatever every hour for about ten minutes and don't let them step off of it. The entire time, you should be repeating and telling them the commands that you've chosen for them to associate with the green light to do their business. Hopefully, this will make them potty on the right surface at least a few times a day. When they do, give them treats and praise them.

As you continue doing this, they'll have fewer and fewer accidents and have more and more success with the pad.

Again, if they have accidents, don't punish them. Instead, simply move them over to the pad as quickly as you can, saying the commands such as "no" if you catch them having the accident. If they finish their business on the pad, reward them same as always.

Eventually, your dog should get to the point where they can roam freely around the house without supervision. They should learn how to find the pad when they need it. This allows you to simply change it out once or twice a day as needed. Also, if you think they need to go, consistently using the same word in the first few weeks of training as you watch them potty will help them associate the "time to go" with that specific sound. Eventually, they'll know this sound so well that they'll go to the pad and relieve themselves whenever they hear it.

Top Potty-Training Tips

Before you even start to begin thinking of how to house train your new Lab pup and how to dip yourself and your dog in to the process to begin teaching it to your pup, there are a few things you can do to start getting them in the right mood and mindset to learn the house training procedure on the day you bring them home. First, you should teach them to respect and obey everyone in your home. This can be done first by making sure they are on good grounds with everyone who is regularly going to be in the home with them or at least in the space they're going to regularly inhabit.

One thing you can do right away to ensure this is making sure that your new Lab pup doesn't act aggressively towards any of these people (you should also make sure that your new Lab pup doesn't act aggressively towards strangers, but this requires them acting amiable towards the people they are around day by day first). It also requires that your new lab pup isn't mistreated by anyone who is regularly in your house as well.

Make sure that everyone in your house knows not to act out with anything but kindness and love towards your new friend. If there is a problem with your new Lab pup's behavior with someone in your house for any reason, you can reconcile the two of them by putting them in a room alone together. Make sure this specific person has plenty of treats that can be used to win over the dog's trust. Then, this person can start playing simple games with the new dog. Playing games with small dogs is a quick way to erase any malice the puppy might have towards them. It is largely a trust-building exercise because in order for a dog to play with someone because it requires the dog to believe that they are in a safe environment with that new person.

Making sure your new Lab pup feels comfortable around everyone in your home ensures that they won't ever feel vulnerable when doing their business because the wrong person comes into their space.

Starting at the beginning, you should know that it is possible to start potty-training dogs too early. While it's never too early to start getting them on a schedule and getting them to associate a certain area with going to the bathroom, intensively training a really young dog to go to the bathroom in the right place can be stressful for them. This is because puppies sixteen weeks or younger have little control over their bladders and other bathroom functions. So if your pup is less than four months old, don't set expectations for them that they can't meet.

As we've discussed before, it's important to get your new Lab puppy on a regular feeding schedule as early as you can. Regulating the time your Lab pup eats will automatically regulate the time they feel the need to do their business. To regulate their schedule, give them a set time to eat. This includes putting food in their dish at the same time as well as taking their bowl away about fifteen minutes after you've given to them. They might be a little hungry between meals at first, but it won't take very long at all for them to learn that they need to eat as much as they need to within that fifteen-minute interval.

You should also take your puppy to the area you want them to do their business in right after when they wake up in the morning and right before when they go to bed at night. You should also take them to that area about thirty minutes after meals as well as about twenty minutes after they drink any water.

You should also make sure you're always encouraging them to do their business in the same spot. Moving their pad around to different locations or taking them outside to different areas will confuse them as to exactly where they should relieve themselves. Keeping the pad in the same spot or taking them out to the same spot will prompt them to go more easily for two reasons: first, the familiarity of the location will relax them as they get more and more into a routine; second, if you bring them to the same place to relieve themselves repeatedly for a good amount of time, the area will build up with their business and it will develop a scent about it that gives them the green light and makes them more comfortable to go. The smell probably won't be palpable to you, but they will be able to sense it.

When training your new Lab pup to do their business outside, if that is what you've chosen to do, make sure you stay with them the entire time they're outside until they're been successfully trained. This is an important thing to do because it makes you new Lab pup feel more comfortable being outside. Also, it makes sure they don't have a chance to run off or get lost because you left them outside when they didn't know better than to run off. Lastly, it ensures you have the chance to watch them to make sure they do their business before you let them back in.

Another good tip for when you're either first starting to or are still in the process of training your pup to do its business outside is to watch them the entire time they're outside and to stay out there with them. Then you keep watching them until they've done their business. As soon as they've done their business, give them either a treat as well as praise or simply just praise depending on what stage they are in their potty-training process. After you've either given them a treat and praise or simply just praise, bring them back inside immediately after they've done their business. This will do two things. The first thing it does is that it makes them associate the praise you're giving them with doing their business outside in the right place. The second thing it does is that it makes the associate getting to go back inside with doing their business outside in the right place.

Another thing you can do to stop them from getting desensitized from the joy they get from getting praise or a treat or both is to give them some other reward for going to the bathroom outside or in the general right place. There are a few different types of awards you can give them in this situation. The rewards that I am going to suggest require that you spend time with your new Lab pup and give them some form of extra attention. One of these awards is simply to take them on a walk in a new environment. This can be as simple as taking them on a walk around the neighborhood your house is in. It can also come in the form of taking them out to a dog park or somewhere new where they can run around and play and have fun without being confined by a leash. It can also come in the form of taking them on a short walk in a nearby forest, either behind your house or close enough to where you live that you can get there on foot in a short amount of time.

When trying to house-train your new Lab pup, you should be aware of the specific needs that your Labrador has as a breed. As they get bigger and stronger, their bladders and the muscles that control them will get bigger and stronger as well. This means that, while it can prevent most accidents, taking you Labrador outside every single hour for ten minutes might end up confusing them because Labs don't need to go to the bathroom as often as some other dogs do. So when you bring them outside when they don't have to go to the bathroom too frequently, it might confuse them as to whether being outside is the sure sign that they are free to go to the bathroom. They should automatically associate being outside with the green light that tells them it's alright to go to the bathroom. Labs are smarter than most other dogs so they'll pick up on this quicker than other breeds will. Still, they don't learn as people do. Be patient with them.

What to Know About Your Labrador's Behavior and How to Control It

L ike all dog breeds, Labrador Retrievers have certain behaviors that are unique to them. In Labradors, you'll see a conglomeration of traits that you probably won't find in any other dog breed. They have specific needs that you should know how to meet. Knowing what traits are common in Labradors and which traits aren't can help you identify the behaviors that are naturally occurring as well as the behaviors that can help you identify certain problems with their physical and mental health.

In this section, I will name and discuss some traits that are definitely behavior traits you should know about your new friend. I will also name and discuss some behavioral traits that might seem innocuous but are still probably things you should be aware of and know how to control. Even small traits can lead to stress for you and your new Lab pup. This stress can manifest in aggressive or other types of unwanted behavior, not eating, or a loss of sleep for both you and your pup.

Most of these traits are inherent in the

Labrador's genetic and evolutionary makeup. it is neither the fault of your dog or the fault of yourself as an owner that your Labrador is displaying these traits. As a result, it is important that you approach correcting these behaviors with both compassion and kindness both for yourself as an owner and for your Labrador as an animal who hasn't really done anything wrong.

Basic Labrador Traits and the Causes of Unwanted Behavior

One of the most recognizable traits of the Labrador Retriever as a dog breed in its kindness and gentleness. Most know or are at least familiar with the Labrador's amiable expression. You don't often see a Labrador who has a scary or negative expression on its face because they're so well known for their good mood. This is part of the reason why that Labradors are often recommended for families that have children because they are often not likely to bite them or act out towards them in other aggressive ways. If your Labrador (or any type of dog breed, for that matter) is acting out aggressively, there's probably something wrong. This isn't to say that you're necessarily a bad owner. It may be that their unwanted behavior is the product of how someone else is acting or treating them or from some other thing that is completely out of your control. It's very possible that they're acting this way because of something that happened to them before you brought them home. It also may be the product of the way someone else is treating them when you're not around.

If your Labrador is exhibiting some kind of aggression or other types of unwanted behavior, you should start figuring out why they're acting that way either immediately or as soon as you possibly can. There are things you may be doing that is causing your new Lab pup to act this way. The list of possible things that could be causing them to act this way is far too long for me to list here, but I will include an example of a case I hear of a while back that embodies some of the more common mistakes that good, loving owners make when otherwise treating their dogs kindly and generally doing everything else right.

A few years ago, I encountered a Labrador that was acting out aggressively towards other people. The owner would put them on a leash and take them out for a walk. On these walks, his Labrador would act out, growling and barking and lunging at certain strangers who would walk by. Also, at home, certain people would come over and the dog would run from them, distance themselves from these certain people and act out towards them with hostility by running around and barking and growling at them.

When I first encountered this Labrador and her owner, I was initially very confused at her behavior. Her owner seemed very put together, calm, and seemed to treat her and other people with respect and kindness. Furthermore, the dog seemed well groomed and well fed and put together. So I spent a while talking to him as to how he was at home with her and which things he often did with her. I was able to point out two problematic things that were causing her to act that way.

First, the man was a big sports fan. He often spent hours a day watching sports games on the TV, specifically hockey and football. He told me that he often got very passionate about the games, perhaps too much so. I asked him to describe to me how he acted while watching them, and he told me, with a bit of embarrassment, that he yelled and screamed and cursed at his TV when things weren't going the way he liked. I asked him if the dog was present during these times, and he said she was. The problem here was that he didn't know that, even if he was not acting this way towards his dog, she was still picking up on his vibe and energy while he was watching these games. Surely, all his yelling and noise got her attention. As he got more and more excited about whatever he was acting out towards, in the same way did she get more and more excited and wired up. The difference is that he, as an emotionally stable human, was able to let go of these powerful emotions after the game ended. But his dog often didn't know that it was time to let go of these emotions as well as how to let go of them, hence that aggression stayed in her and caused her to act out towards other people.

The other thing that was causing this aggression in her took place on the walks he took with her almost daily. He'd take her around the city for about an hour before going back up to his apartment. At the end of these walks, he'd let her off the leash and let her run up the stairs by herself. Then he'd follow her up and wrestle with her at the top of the stairs by the door. While this may seem innocuous, in the sense of how the dog's psyche works, it was very significant. Dogs have an idea of their home space (the apartment at the top of the stairs in this case) as their own and something that must be defended at all cost. By letting her off the leash and letting her run up the stairs, she was taught to retake her home at the end of each of these walks. To make things worse, his wrestling with her was to her a form of fighting for the home. So she was put in this perpetual mindset of having to reclaim and fight for her home every time she went on these walks. This wired her up and made her very defensive of both her owner and her home, which caused her to act out to people she viewed, for whatever reason, as a threat to either of these things.

That story is a good example of how an otherwise good and kind Labrador owner can evoke some kind of aggressive behavior in their Labrador from the simple reason of not understanding both the nature of the dog's mind and how they pick up on the behavior and vibe of both their owners and others around them. So if your dog is displaying some kind of unwanted behavior and you don't know why, I encourage you to analyze everything you do with your dog or the things you do while your dog is present and think about those activities in terms of how they may affect your dog. You cannot cure a dog of any behavior when you don't know the root problem.

Curbing Biting, Licking, and Aggressive Behavior

Biting (often play-biting) and licking are two of the most common problems in all types of dog breeds. In this section, we'll start by looking at why dogs bite and what you can do to curb it. Then we'll move onto biting and describe and cover the same things.

All puppies bite people, either strangers or the person they're closest to you. A lot of owners don't see play-biting as a huge problem, but a lot of people are very put off at the idea of a dog covering their hand with saliva and all the germs that come with it. To keep yourself from putting people who might come into contact with your dog with this problem, it's useful to know just how to stop your dog from doing it.

Play-biting is common in dogs up to the age of about eighteen months. While it can be cute and non-painful when the dog is very tiny, this can change when the dog gets bigger and stronger. Now, your dog is biting in the same way that it did when it was a little puppy, only now it hurts and it's more than just an occasional nuisance.

There are a couple of main reasons that puppies

bite. The first is that they have new teeth coming in, and sometimes this can be quite uncomfortable for them. Biting can help decrease the uncomfortableness they feel as their new teeth come in as well as toughen up their teeth. Biting also serves as a way for them to play and manipulate objects. If you try to get your dog to not bite anything, you're probably going to have a rough time because biting is the way they eat and experience the world. So it's very important that you supply them with an object that they're allowed to bite such as ropes, stuffed animals, bones, or chew-toys.

Some biting is to be expected from your new Lab pup. But there are a lot of reasons that your new Lab up might be either biting more than you'd like or continuing to bite a lot after they're biting at an age where they're older than they should be. A lot of times this is because they're getting more excited than they can handle and it causes them to do things that they have some idea that they shouldn't. In fact, most problems that people experience with puppies is often due to them being more excited than they know how to handle.

When a puppy bites because they're over-excited, there's usually a few things that come along with it. These things include growling or snarling, running around and stopping and going very quickly in jolting fashion, nipping at you or someone else in a very quick, hyper manner (the zoomies), ripping your clothes or their toys, fast wagging of the tail, or spinning around very quickly.

So what should you do if your puppy is overly excited? Well, if it's clear that they're overly-excited, there are a few things you should do immediately. First, you should look at how you're playing with your Lab puppy and end the game as soon as possible. Second, put the Lab puppy in a space that is quiet and free from distractions or anything else that could possibly get them excited. Also, if you can or if you want to or feel like you need to, you can leave the space and leave them by themselves for a little while. This will result in a lack of stimuli for your Lab pup and is a quick way to get them to calm down. After they've gotten calmed down and they're not nipping or acting out anymore, you should analyze what you were doing with your lab pup before they starting biting and acting overly excited and search for things that may have triggered it. Take an honest look at the situation and think of what you can do differently in the future to prevent this. This doesn't mean that, if your Lab puppy got overly excited at a certain game, that you can or should never play that game with them again. It simply means that the next time you play that game with your Lab pup, you should tone down the intensity of the game you're playing.

You should know how to tell the difference as to whether or not your pup's biting is the result of being overly excited or whether it is the result of them being aggressive. Even if your pup is loud and running around a lot, chances are it's from simply being overly excited. Something you should know about aggression is that it's almost always a result of your dog being afraid. When a dog is aggressive, it usually gets very still or at most will pace or make short movements, always going back into the same posture and focusing on the same point. Dogs that afraid of something don't run all over the room. Another sure way to tell if your dog is aggressive is the position of their tail. Usually, it will be between their legs. Often a scared and aggressive dog will act scared and fearfully, and as a result, they'll hide in corners or beneath furniture or freeze in place completely.

If you catch your dog being aggressive towards you or anyone, immediately isolate them from the situation. Take them into a safe place where there aren't a lot of people or things that could scare them in any sense. Try getting some of their favorite treats and hold them out to them or throw them on the ground. Do not try to pet your dog or move near it quickly. Make your motions very slow and gentle and speak to your dog in a comforting tone. It might take a while for your dog to calm down and trust you. After you've gotten them to calm down, keep them in a safe place where they can relax. Then you should take an honest assessment of the situation and what made them scared and caused them to act aggressively. Do everything you can to avoid putting your dog in that situation again and educate anyone who was involved not to act in whatever way they did towards your lab again.

If your dog is acting aggressively and there

doesn't seem to be any obvious reason for it, take them to the vet. It is possible that they have some sort of injury or condition that is causing them pain. Dogs can't tell us that they aren't feeling good or that they're in pain. When dogs are hurt or they have something that's causing them pain, they often act out aggressively in fear of being hurt more.

Licking is almost never the product of aggression, which makes it far less worrying than biting. But having a dog that licks excessively or obsessively can be a burden. When a dog licks you, all the bacteria in their mouth (which probably has thousands, if not millions, of contaminates) gets onto your skin, which is pretty gross to think about.

Dogs lick for two main reasons. The first reason they lick is also found among wolves and other animals in the wild. These wild animals lick because it shows submission to the dominant animals in the group. They also lick because it shows affection towards their peers in the group. So, when a dog licks you, there's a good chance that they're doing it as a sign of affections and that you're in control and they trust you.

But dogs sometimes also lick because of the simple reason that they like the taste of your skin. If you don't know why, do a simple experiment and lick your arm. It tastes salty, right? Your sweat glands produce water that is very high in salt, sodium, and other minerals. Dogs usually like this salty taste and so that's why they like to lick you. A simple way of getting your dog to stop licking you is to get them a salt lick. Most dog food doesn't have a lot of sodium, and so most dogs are at least a little low in sodium. Getting them a salt rock or other types of salt licks that they can lick whenever they want is a good way to increase your dog's sodium levels and decrease the amount that they feel the need to lick you.

When a dog licks because of affection, it makes them feel good. Their brains produce endorphins that evoke feelings of pleasure and trust. One sure way to combat this form of licking is to eliminate the endorphins they get from licking. So how do we decrease the endorphins? It's simple; never react positively to licking. Licking should never be rewarded. If your Lab licks you, ignore them. Talk to them in a stern voice and don't praise them. You can even get up and move to the other room. This won't work right away. It might take them a while to learn that licking results in things that aren't positive and are even things that they don't like. This is why it's important to be consistent. Don't budge. Don't give in and reward them for it. Make it clear to them that if they lick you, they will not be rewarded.

Curbing Barking

All Labradors bark. It's just going to happen. But there's a difference between a Lab that barks occasionally at understandably intense stimuli and a dog that barks constantly. A Lab that barks too much can be very disruptive to not only the owners of the dog but also to the neighbors and anyone who might come over to your home. Knowing how to effectively and kindly stop a dog from barking is one of the best things you can do for both the atmosphere of your home as well as the relationship your dog has both with you and as well as everyone your dog comes into contact with.

It's important that your dog knows when it is okay to bark and as well as when it's important for them to be quiet. If your dog barks excessively, it's your job as someone who chose to bring your dog into your neighborhood to keep it from disturbing and annoying those around your home. As soon as you realize that your dog is barking too much, you should start working to reverse that habit immediately before it becomes deeply ingrained into your dog's personality. One way you can curb barking is to teach your dog commands that tell it to speak and tell it to be quiet.

The first step to curbing your Labrador's excessive barking is understanding why it's barking so much. There can be a variety of reasons why your dog is barking too much. I'll list them shortly below.

Territorial Barking: This is barking that stems from the need your dog feels to protect you as well as their home. This comes in the form of barking at animals as well as strangers who may come into or close to their home. My Labrador, who has a yard to run around in without a fence (I live very far out in the country), often barks at night at wild animals such as coyotes or raccoons.

Lonely Barking: Dogs function best and are their happiest when they're surrounded by other animals or people that they feel close to (think of the term "pack"). When Labradors are alone for much of the day, it tends to make them very unhappy. They like to be with other dogs or people. Like us, they need others to have a sense of fulfillment. When they're not happy, they tend to bark out of a lack of happiness.

"Hello" Barking: This is probably the healthiest form of barking. Barking is basically how dogs talk. When they meet someone new, whether they're happy to meet them or suspicious of them, it's their instinct to bark at them.

Separation Anxiety Barking: This often takes place in very young puppies. When a dog is very young (around four months or younger), their natural instinct is to want to be around their mother or whoever is taking care of them. So they sometimes have a real problem with being alone, especially when they're about to go to sleep at night. We won't cover this here but in one of the other sections of this chapter.

Attention-Seeking Barking: Sometimes Labradors bark for attention. This can vary as to which attention level is so low that your dog feels the need to bark. If your Labrador is used to a high level of attention, then it's going to take less of a lack of attention to get them to bark.

Pain Barking: Sometimes, when dogs have medical issues that cause them pain, dogs will bark to voice their discontent.

The best thing you can do to curb excessive barking is to figure out the cause of excessive barking and remove it from the equation. Along with this, there is something you don't want to do, which is to encourage barking in any way. Encouraging barking, even when you don't mean to, will make it very confusing for your Labrador when you try to curb their barking.

You can start by making sure your dog is very active. Do your best to make sure they're tired by the time they go to bed at night. Go in walks, play games with them, or do anything else you can to burn them out of having energy by the end of the day. A dog that is kept up all day will have a lot of energy when it gets dark and it is time to go to bed. A tired dog is a quiet dog.

You should also try to make sure that your dog has company. The lonely dog is a loud dog. They act out for attention. Make sure your dog gets attention and is satisfied with their environment.

One thing you should never do is to reward your

dog when they're barking. Often good-meaning Labrador owners accidentally encourage excessive barking by thinking their dog needs to be coaxed into being quiet. If you think that your dog is barking because it's lonely, don't go out and try to give it company right away. Do it the next day or sometime when they're not barking. If you go out and try to comfort your barking dog, you're rewarding their behavior. This will teach them to bark to get rewards, which you do not want.

You also should not act negatively towards your dog for barking. Don't shout or scream at them for barking. This will add to their excitement and perhaps will make them bark more.

If you find your dog barking excessively, there are a few things you can do to try to stop it right away. You can throw them a toy or give them a nice snack to avert their attention. You can also command them to sit down, come, or do any other thing that will get their attention off whatever they're barking at.

As a long-term solution when none of these reasons seem to explain why your dog is barking and it's a chronic problem, you can train your dog commands of when to speak and be quiet.

How to Deal with Separation Anxiety

Separation Anxiety is one of the most common problems in Labradors. It doesn't just take place in puppies, but dogs of all ages. It can also manifest itself in dogs of any age. Separation Anxiety can be very destructive, not just to your dogs physical and mental health but also can be a detriment to their mental health. If they freak out when they're left alone, they can do some serious damage to your furniture and other objects around the house. You've probably seen photos of dogs sulking around cushions, pillows, trash bags, or other things they've ripped apart. Sometimes this kind of destruction can be caused by your Lab's simple bad behavior, but more often it is caused by the distress they feel when their owners are not around. In this section, we'll cover the causes on Separation Anxiety as well as things you can do for your dog to eliminate this behavior.

This kind of behavior could be because they don't know which objects around them are okay to chew on and which are not. But more often it's simple separation anxiety. A good way to determine which it is by watching how your dog behaves as you're getting ready to leave the house without them. If they seem calm and uninterested, it may not be separation anxiety that's causing their behavior. However, if your dog acts sad or nervous when you are getting ready to leave, that's a sign of separation anxiety. Some dogs with separation anxiety will even try to stop their owners from leaving. Another way to tell whether or not your Lab has separation anxiety is to wait outside after you leave and listen for the sounds inside. If your dog is whining or barking directly after you've left them alone, that's a good sign that they have separation anxiety. They may also go to the bathroom inside the house when left alone. Some dogs may even try to escape the area they're confined in if their separation anxiety is too much for them to handle.

There are a few different causes of separation anxiety. It is known that dogs that come from a shelter or some type of abusive environment are more likely to develop separation anxiety. Another common cause of separation anxiety is the loss of another pet or of an important person who was previously around their home a lot. It can also develop when a dog's schedule changes drastically. For example, if they're used to being left alone from seven until three and then you switch to second shift and are gone from three to twelve, they could get thrown off of what they're used to and become very confused as to when their owner is coming back. Another thing that can cause separation anxiety is when they've moved from one place to another which puts the dog in a new environment and confuses them. It can also be caused by a new person moving into the home, putting them on edge by having a person they don't know being around a lot. It can also just be a product of having a dog that's too young to know better.

Also, when a dog is left in a room without something to entertain itself with, it can cause destruction, go to the bathroom, and try to escape out of boredom alone. If your dog is behaving like this and is locked in a room without a window, toys, or a friend to play with for an extended amount of time, try putting them into a place where they have something that can occupy their mind before you decide it's separation anxiety.

There are a few things you can do to help your dog with separation anxiety. If your dog's separation anxiety isn't too bad (but still a problem), something you can do is to do things that make them associate being alone with something that makes them happy. One possible course of action is to give them some sort of delicious food when you leave. You should give them enough of the treat that it will take them a while to eat all of it. Another thing you can do to help your Lab with separation anxiety is to get a kind of toy that requires the dog to work to get to the inside. You can put some sort of a tasty treat inside it that they'll have to work to get out. It can be a type of chew toy that requires them to chew on it for quite a while (maybe even a few hours) before they can get to the tasty food inside. This will do two things; first, it will help them associate the tasty treat with being alone for an extended amount of time; second, it will give them something to entertain themselves with while you're gone, helping them get their mind off the fact that they're alone.

If your dog's separation anxiety is more severe and is causing serious problems both to your home and to your Lab's health, there are some more time-consuming steps you should take to rectify this problem. One thing you can do is to decrease the time they're alone until you find a period that they're comfortable with. If you aren't capable of coming back to your home this often for whatever reason, try to find a family member or a friend that can stop by every so often to visit your dog and put them at ease. As they get used to being alone for these short periods of time, slowly start extending the period they are in the home alone until they get to the point where they can be alone for the entire time you have to be gone.

Teaching Your Labrador How to Fetch

When you think of a Labrador and their owner playing in a park, you probably imagine them playing fetch. Fetch is one of the best, most classical game you can play with your dog. It's an incredibly good bonding experience as well as being a great way to keep your dog fit and active. But most dogs don't know how to play fetch, and probably as many owners don't know how to teach them to. Everyone loves a Lab that can play fetch. They're usually friendly, well-adjusted, and knowing how to fetch gives them a sure way to bond with anyone who might cross into your life. In this section, we'll go over when to start teaching your dog how to fetch, the basic training methods you can start with, and some techniques you can do to perfect the game.

Basic Methods to Start With

To be honest, a dog is really never too young to start learning something. However, it should be done in the right way with realistic expectations. Young Labs have short attention spans and, especially in the first few months, may not have the cognitive ability or the energy to learn a game as intensive and fetching. Don't get me wrong, it's much easier to teach young dogs than old dogs, but, if you do start training your Lab pup when it's only a few months old, be prepared to spend more time training them than you would if they were around six months old.

Dogs will never know how to fetch unless you teach them how to correctly. It's not instinctual. While they are often automatically inclined to chase after and run off with something you've thrown, there's nothing that tells them to bring it back to you. Teaching a dog how to return what you've thrown to you is the hardest part of teaching a dog how to fetch. Every step along the path to mastering the game of fetch is a challenge for your dog. They have to learn and think and change their own behavior.

Something you can do to start the process of teaching them to fetch from a very young age is by simply throwing a ball, stick, or another toy, waiting for them to pick it up, and then chasing them as they run around with it. The game "chase" is something dogs love to do and will almost always do automatically. They love to chase. However, if your dog doesn't seem interested, something you can do is to offer them a reward for retrieving the object, practicing throwing it near and far over and over again until they develop an interest in it. When the pick it up, give them a treat. Even if he just goes over near it and smells it without picking it up, give him a treat and award them for showing interest in it. Do this over and over again until they run over and pick up the object every single time. If you're having a hard time getting them interested, try restricting their movement right after you throw it. Like teenagers, the fastest thing you can do to get a dog interested in something is to make them think you don't want them to do it.

Now that you've taught your dog to chase after and pick up the object consistently, it's important to do as much as you can to keep them focused. A big problem people run into when teaching their dog how to fetch is that the dog just wants to grab the object and run around with it. It might be funny at first, but soon you'll get tired of chasing your Lab around trying to get the object back. So a good way to help keep your dog within your reach is to use a long leash or rope to reel them in when they get too excited and simply don't want to give the object back to you. If you don't have a leash or a rope long enough, something else you can do is offer them a treat when they're running around with the object. Usually, when your Lab sees the food, they'll drop the object and come over to get the treat. If they try to pick up the object and run with it, gently pull on the rope and then start running or walking in the other direction. When you do this, your dog will come over to you.

When they come over to you, praise them and get them a treat. Doing this will encourage them to come over to you in the future.

Another problem many people run into when teaching their Labs how to fetch is that their dogs want to play tug-of-war with you for the object. Most dogs love this game, and often they'll hold onto it with every muscle they have for a very long time. In the same way as above, you can offer them a treat to get them to let it go. Put the treat right by their nose so they can smell it. Usually, they'll let go of the object to get the treat.

Mastering the Game

After you can get your dog to consistently pick up the treat and you have a way of getting it back with ease, you can start training them to do the hardest part of fetching which is retrieving.

There's a big difference between a dog that knows how to fetch and a dog that can only run after an object and claim it as its own. Retrieving is going to take the longest amount of time to train your dog how to do than any other part of the process of learning fetching will. When you first start trying to teach them this, it can be a very long and hard and frustrating process. But it's important to keep your cool and to treat your dog with nothing but kindness, patience, and compassion. Learning how to fetch should not be a stressful experience for your dog. If they feel nervous or distressed, it will make all of your play time a time they don't want to be apart of. It can also manifest itself in other behavioral problem at home or with other dogs or people.

When you first start trying to teach them this stage of fetching, they probably won't have any interest in bringing the object back at all. What can help you here is to get a second toy to get their attention and make them drop the object. You can do this either by throwing it or teasing them with it. Once they've expressed interest in the second toy, they'll likely drop the first toy. You can try going over and picking it up, keeping their interest in the second toy if you can. This way your Lab has no toys while you have both, which you can use in the exact same way if they don't want to bring the first toy back at all again. This also gets your lab used to the idea of running back to you after they've picked up the object. Any time your Lab comes back over to you after picking up the object, even if they hold onto the toy or try running away again, give them a treat. It makes them associate getting a treat with the act of bringing the object back to you.

As you try to teach them the act of retrieving, call their name when right after they pick up the object. It helps if your dog already knows and can consistently obey the command for "come" in other circumstances. Teaching a dog to fetch should usually be done only after a dog has been taught how to do other commands. It helps reduce the chances that your Lab will run away from you or be generally difficult while trying to teach them to fetch.

If your dog begins to bring the object back over to you but drops it before they come over to you all the way, say "bring it here" or "give it here." Do this every time they retrieve it, whether they bring it all the way back to you or not. Also, if they drop it, go over and pick it up and then walk back to the place where you were standing before throwing the object again. This will help them when they don't understand. Once you've done it enough, only throw the object from a certain area and that's where you need to be with the object to throw it again.

You should also make sure that you're playing

catch with something your dog likes and has interest in. If you get a random stick that they haven't shown interest in, it's going to be hard to get them interested enough in it to go over and pick it up. If you're having trouble getting your dog interested, experiment with different types of toys such as bones or small balls until you've found something they want to go get and don't want to let go of.

Leash Training Your Labrador

Proper leash training is one of the most important things you can teach your dog. It should also be one of the first things you try to teach your dog. A dog that knows how to properly behave when they're on the leash can be the difference between a dog whose walks are tiring and stressful and a dog whose walks are relaxing and casual. It also saves you from embarrassment from walking a dog that barks at people or tries to flee from you when you're out in public. You can always tell when a dog hasn't been properly leash trained. They're always pulling their owners with a lot of force and stopping to sniff things with no regards to what their owner wants to do, causing their owner to have to either won't until their done or to yank them with what is probably more force than they would like to use.

In this section, we'll go over why dogs misbehave on the leash, the difference between good leash behavior and bad leash behavior, and what you can do to train your dog to behave correctly on the leash when out and about. Following the steps in this section should teach your dog how to keep going without you trying to pull them, how to go around corners and follow your direction, and how to walk by people and other animals without misbehaving.

Bad Leash Behavior

One of the most common problems with leash behavior is pulling on the leash. The reasons why Labs pull on leashes is very simple. Like all dogs, Labs have a natural instinct to not give in to pressure. Instead, they almost always feel the need to pull against it. When they're restricted by a leash, they're going to want to go places outside of the space they're allotted. They also want to get to where they're going faster (most humans move a lot slower when they're walking than dogs would like). When labs are on the leash, they're usually not focused on the human on the other end. They're in their old world. This can lead to some nerve-racking problems such as choking which can scare owners since their dogs cough, heave, and gasp. But this reaction usually sounds worse than it really is.

Another problem people often experience when walking their dogs is that their Labs like to bite or chew on the leash. How often labs do this depend on the individual dog. Some dogs do it just because they like it. Other dogs only do it because they're overly nervous or excited. Another reason Labs chew or bite on the leash is because they want attention, as biting or chewing on the leash often makes their owners react in some way.

A dog that isn't leash-trained will also do a lot of stopping. The root of this problem is similar to the problem that causes dogs to pull on the leash. They do this because they don't have a sense of a connection with the human on the other end of the leash. Again, they're in their old little world, and, when they see or smell something interesting, their natural inclination is a powerful desire to stop and observe it.

How to Fix Bad Leash Behavior

Something you should be able to do before ever taking them out on a walk is the ability to take their attention no matter where the two of you are. They should be able to react to their name and obey commands no matter what place they find themselves in. You can start practicing this by calling their name in your home or in any other place that doesn't have any distractions. After they can do this consistently, try going out into the yard or into another place that has slightly more distractions. As they get better and better at doing this easily, move them into bigger, busier environments. This is the first step in correcting bad behavior.

One of the other things you should do early in the process is to learn to control the environments you take your Lab on walks on as best as you can. Taking them on walks with loud traffic can make it harder for them to hear you when you need to give them some sort of commands. It can also cause them to be over-excited and unable to obey your commands or calm down. Also, depending on whether or not your lab is trained to be calm and comfortable around dogs, you should make sure you're not taking them into an environment where they might be overwhelmed with and act out at other dogs. If you do find yourself approaching a dog and your lab is not reacting well or isn't ready for being around another dog, go in a half circle around the dog to keep the dog and your Lab at a safe distance from one another.

If your dog has a problem with barking while the two of you are on walks, there's probably a simple, easy to fix reason for this. Most excessive barking is usually caused by simply having too much energy. If you find your dog barking at people or other animals, try playing a game that will wear him out before you leave the house. You can play chase, tug-of-war, or any other kind of game that will make them tired after a while. Exercising not only keeps your Lab in good health, but it also has a calming effect on them after they've done it. It takes a lot of energy to act out with bad behavior. A tired dog is a calm dog.

A good way to stop your dog from pulling is by enacting strict leash discipline. For example, the only time your dog should be allowed to move ahead of you is when the leash isn't strained. As soon as it tightens, stop walking and don't budge. Wait for the dog to move back a little and loosen the leash before letting the two of you move forward again. It may take a while for your Lab to change his behavior by doing this, but it's worth it once they learn. If you're having a particularly hard time changing your lab's behavior, you can come up with a command to say every time you have to stop for pulling on the leash. Eventually, this should get to the point where your Lab will stop pulling on the leash from that command alone.

It is also a very big help if you've previously trained your dog to respond to basic commands. This is because, if your dog stops to smell or look at something, one thing you can do to rectify their behavior is to ask them to do a basic command to get their attention off whatever object they're smelling or looking at.

Another thing you can do to get your dog to stop their bad leash behavior is to train them to be aware and attentive to you on their walks. All you have to do to get this behavior instilled in them is to carry a good amount of treats with you while you're on walks with them. Pay attention to where they're looking. Every time they look back at you on the walk, give them a treat or a reward. If your dog isn't looking at you at all, call their name and give them a treat when they look at you. This gets your Lab to associate looking at you with the pleasure of getting a treat. It can make them, over time, if done consistently, very in tune with whoever is walking them. It can make them very respectful and thoughtful as to what the person who's walking them is doing.

If your dog has a problem with biting or chewing on their leash while walking, one thing you can do is to take the focus off the act of chewing or biting on the leash and replacing it with something else. Find some other behavior to reward, such as certain kinds of walks. Of course, this means that your dog must already know other types of walks before this kind of discipline can work. Another thing you can do to fix this behavior if your Lab doesn't know any other kinds of commands to replace with leash biting or chewing is to take away the reason they're biting or chewing on a leash. This can be done by walking them with two leashes. When the Lab starts to bit or chew on one leash, drop it and use the other. Once the leash goes loose, they likely won't be interested in chewing or biting on it anymore.

Maintaining Your Labrador's Behavior

It is not much good to train your dog how to behave well and how to do all these commands and tricks if they lose the ability how to do it after a couple of months. You can't spend a few months training your dog and then just drop off the amount of effort you put in. This is because training does a couple things for a Lab. First, it gives it order and structure. It makes it feel like it has a purpose, and Labs who feel as though they have a purpose are much happier and much more well behaved than those that don't. Second, it keeps your dog in good physical health by making sure it has plenty of exercises. Third, it provides both of you with a bonding experience. The dynamic you form with your dog by teaching them commands as well as having them execute commands keeps the two of you on the same page. You become very in tune as to what their current mood is and your Lab becomes very in tune to your mood.

Maintaining Good Behavior

An important part of learning good behavior is that it instills in the Lab the difference between which behaviors are good and which behaviors are bad. Of course, you don't go through and teach them every single bad behavior. Instead, you give them a certain command that you can use at any time when they exhibit bad behavior. It's important that you use this consistently. The longer you use it, the more receptive they will be towards it. It will make them stop the behavior quicker and quicker as time goes on. Do not let bad behavior slide by, no matter how inane it may seem. Once they get away with something, they then think it's alright. When they think something's alright, they do it again. Not only do they do it again, but they then push it further. It can be easy to slip into the habit of letting some of your dog's seemingly unimportant bad behavior slip by because you think it isn't a big deal, and that one incident probably isn't. but once you've let it slip once, it's easier to let it slip the next time. Also, it can cause stress to your Lab because you're sending them mixed messages. If something seems okay to do half the time and not okay the other half of the time, they won't know which one to do and that can cause distress when you do scold them for it.

Because of what we've described above, you always need to be giving your dog feedback, and it shouldn't just be in response to bad behavior. Instead, just like you discourage bad behavior, you should always be encouraging good behavior. When your Lab showcases its training or does something right or really well, they should know that what they've just done is good.

This doesn't mean you have to always give them a few treats, but it does mean that you should show your appreciation of the good behavior.

You should also exercise the right kind of behavior in the right times and places. If there's one place you should be exercising your control over your dog's behavior, it should be in an exciting, stimulating, or challenging situations. If you bring your dog to a dog park, and there's a dog there that your Lab isn't acting positively towards, you should tell them to sit or get their attention, keeping their behavior in check and making sure they can continuously focus on you in these kinds of environments. Another place your dog's good behavior should be tested is in the home when you have company over. You should always make sure your dog is calm and non-aggressive towards anyone who walks in your house. If they are, you should immediately get them under control and put them into a different room where they can calm down.

One of the most important things you can do to maintain your Lab's good behavior is to make sure that they are healthy and happy. When a dog is getting too little of something it needs or too much of something it doesn't, this excess or deficiency can often manifest itself in bad behavior. There are many different aspects of your dog's life you should keep a close eye on to keep them balanced.

First, you should make sure your dog is getting enough food and water and general nutrients. Second, you should make sure your dog is getting enough social activity, either with you or other animals. You really don't want to leave your dog alone for long periods of time (more than four hours) if you can help it. If you don't have a choice in this matter, put it in a yard with plenty of space or a dog daycare center. If you have no choice but to keep your dog inside, they should at the very least have a window to look out of. Also, if they have to be inside, give them a dog toy designed to keep their interest such as a food-holder they have to chew through to get the snack or some sort of puzzle. You should also make sure your dog is living in an environment that is as stress-free as it can possibly be. Recall the story I told of a dog who was on edge because of how her owner reacted to sports games. As far as you can help it, you should make sure your home is calm and quiet.

Maintaining Your Lab's Training

Like how a car needs to have oil changes and tune-ups to keep running well, in the same way does a Lab need constant upkeep to keep their training sharp and crisp. You should have your

Lab practicing its tricks daily, even if it's only a few. A good way to remember to do this is to have a ritual you do with your dog every day. When you feed them, you can have them sit patiently while you put down the food and then have them speak before they eat. Also, when letting them in and out of the house, you can practice the "come" and "sit" and "speak commands. If you're into exercising and have the time for it, you can bring your dog on a nightly walk and have them practice good leash training as well as obedience around things that may excite or over-stimulate them. You can also take them to a dog park or open field and play a daily game of fetch with them, practicing come, sit, and go commands in between throws. Maintaining this training is also a good way to make sure your Lab stays the same.

Another good thing you can do to maintain your Lab's training is to keep challenging them.

Besides the basic commands and games, there are also hundreds of different games and commands you can teach to your dog beside the ones we've covered. Constantly teaching your dog different commands has a few positive benefits. First, it keeps their mind sharp by challenging them with new things they don't know how to do. Second, it keeps a nice, strong bond between the two of you by ensuring you spend so much time with them giving them your attention. Third, it keeps them focused on you. One of the worst things that can happen in terms of training your dog is for your dog to stop being attentive towards you. This can come about because you're not practicing your commands enough or because your dog gets bored with certain things. Constantly adding more commands makes your dog excited and interested in the time you spend together.

Besides teaching your Lab new skills, you can

also practice the same old skills in new situations and environments. If your dog has mastered the basic commands at home, take them on hikes and into new places they haven't been to before. Get their interest peaked and then practice those old commands in places they're excited to be in. Practice taking him around people and practice those commands with them there. This will increase your Lab's attention span. When a dog's in an environment with lots of interesting things around, it's harder for them to focus on what you're saying. So bringing them into these kinds of environments and practicing these skills will make them a lot more attentive towards you and, as a result, easier to control.

If your dog does lose its training, don't challenge them too much. Slowly move your way back to the basics to see what your lab's skill level is. Once you find it, work up from there. It's not necessarily a bad thing that your dog loses training, it just means you get to spend more time with them in order to retrain them. They'll almost definitely learn faster than before.

Socializing Your Labrador

Even if your Lab is an only dog and you live in a rural area far away from other dogs, you should always make sure you socialize your dog. Chances are your dog is going to come into close contact with another dog at least once in its life. Your dog should also learn how to meet other people without acting badly.

Properly training them how to react and act around other dogs and people can be the difference between a short, peaceful encounter and your dog acting aggressively and getting hurt.

When your dog meets another person or dog, there are two things you don't want them to do. First, you don't want them to act aggressively toward it. Barking doesn't always mean aggression, but growling usually does. It may also be that the other dog may not be properly socialized, and if that's the case, you want to be able to maintain control over your dog in order to remove them from the situation and get them to safety. You also don't want them to be so scared their tail is between their legs.

If your Lab is this nervous, other dogs will pick up on it as well and may perhaps get defensive or act out aggressively. You never want to be the owner of the aggressive or otherwise anti-social dog. In this section, I'll provide you with the steps you can take to do as much as you can to make sure your dog behaves healthily and is comfortable around other dogs. I'll also go through a method for socializing them as well as some extra tips.

Meeting Other Dogs

Your Lab will be most easily socialized when they're puppies, and there are different things you should do to socialize dogs at different ages, but we'll start with puppies.

Lab puppies are the easiest to socialize because everything is still new to them, meaning they're not yet completely used to being the only dog around. Like college kids, young Labs are highly open to new experiences, and they're more likely to approach things with curiosity rather than aggression. The best thing you can do to socialize your puppy with other dogs is to expose them to dogs. You should make sure the dogs you're exposing them to are safe and non-aggressive, as little as one bad experience can sour them to other dogs for the rest of their lives. Go to clubs for dog enthusiasts as these places are more likely to have experienced, dedicated dog owners whose dogs don't react negatively to other dogs. Do this often, as most dogs that are aggressive to other dogs are aggressive because they haven't been exposed to other dogs as puppies.

Socializing an adolescent Lab to be around other dogs is harder than it is to socialize a puppy, but still easier than socializing a full grown adult dog. The only way to socialize a Lab is to expose it to other dogs. Adolescent dogs are more likely to react negatively to new dogs than puppies, which is why it's important not to expose them to too many dogs too quickly. They also shouldn't immediately have dogs directly near them. A good place to socialize Labs of these ages is at the dog park. Dog parks usually have plenty of space, and surely there will be an area within it where you can play with your dog while not having other dogs too near it. While your dog probably won't act out aggressively, chances are they will be frightened. It is important that you don't punish your dog for being frightened. You should also be sure not to put them into situations they can't handle which may overwhelm them. Start slow. Bring your Lab closer and closer to other dogs while giving them time to adjust. If they begin to react negatively, move back and wait for them to calm down. Chances are they won't be completely socialized the first time. You'll have to commit to the process of socializing your dog for a few weeks.

Adult Labs are the hardest to socialize. Adult Labs that aren't used to other dogs are the most likely dogs to act aggressively when around other dogs. Since puppies and adolescent dogs must be exposed to other dogs as the only way to keep them socialized, in the same way, there's no other way to socialize an adult dog with other dogs besides than to expose it to them. Just because your adult dog isn't socialized or has reacted negatively to other dogs in the past doesn't mean it has to be deprived of the company its whole life. Adult dogs that aren't socialized must be introduced to other dogs very slowly. This means pushing them very slowly. Try just going on walks in areas where they may see other dogs from a distance. Go to dog parks weekly, keeping your distance from other dogs until you are completely sure your dog can handle going closer. You can also take it to new places at a slow pace. Try taking it to a new place once a week. You may also try to introduce it to other activities around other dogs at the same rate. It may take a while, but your dog will eventually get socialized. If you are worried about your dog acting aggressively, you should consider getting them a muzzle to wear around other dogs until you're sure they can handle it.

Meeting New People

In the same way a dog must meet other dogs to be comfortable around other dogs, your dog must meet new people to be comfortable around new people.

Puppies have the easiest time becoming socialized with other dogs as well as people. There aren't very many puppies who treat new people with hostility because they don't feel the need to be suspicious towards other people. The best thing you can do to socialize your dog towards other people is to have them meet people as often as possible. The more often your dog meets people, the easier it will be for them. There isn't much you have to do to facilitate this.

Puppies love everyone and everyone loves puppies.

When your dog gets older without gaining experience in meeting other people, however, meeting people can be intimidating for them and problematic. New people and unfamiliar faces can make older dogs nervous when they're not used to seeing new faces. There are a few things you can do to help facilitate this process and make your Lab more comfortable meeting new people. The first thing you can do is to introduce them to one person at a time. Don't try to overwhelm your Lab by bringing in a bunch of people at once. They'll freak out and act negatively. The second thing you can do is to warn the person you're introducing them so that they should come in slowly and quietly and gently. Coming in with a calm vibe can help an older dog get comfortable quicker with a new person. You should make sure the dog gets familiar with the person by smelling them and perhaps getting petted by them. But don't let the person just walk over to them. Let the dog approach the person. You should always let your Lab meet people at its own pace.

Extra Games and Commands to Teach Your Labrador

O nce you Lab has a good grasp over the basic commands and knows a few fun games to play, it can be fun and helpful for both of you to teach it new commands and games. It keeps your time together interesting and fun. Constantly learning new commands and games can help your dog stay sharp and alert. It also makes you a better owner as you come to a deeper understanding of your dog's behavior. Also, it strengthens the bond between the two of you. Teaching your dog new commands and games can also keep your dog glued to you. When a dog is challenged by something you give it, it's going to focus on you more and more to overcome it. A Lab that's constantly learning new games and commands has a much larger attention span than other dogs.

In this section, I'll give you some fun, interesting new commands, and games that you can play and do with your dog. However, before you start trying to do these things with your dog, you should make sure your dog has mastered and can consistently do all the basic commands. This ensures you can keep your dog from getting distracted as well as ensuring that they have the ability to pay close attention to your words and actions.

New Commands

The "off" command. This is a useful command if you have a Lab that likes to jump up on people to say high. It's a command that basically tells them to move away from you. You can do this command by holding a treat in your hand and keeping it closed. You get hold your hand down against your dog's nose. They'll sniff it and eventually move back once they realize that the hand is closed. As they do this, say "off." When they've moved all the way back, give them a treat. Do this over and over again until you can get them to move back with the simple command.

The "out" command. This command is meant to simply make the dog get something out of their mouth. It can be learned by playing the simple game of tug-of-war. You don't need treats to teach them this one. Get a rope or something else the two of you can play tug-of-war with and have them bite it and then try to take it away from them. Play for a while and don't let them win. Instead, keep pulling on it until you Lab lets go. As soon as it's out of their mouth, say out. Do this over and over again until they drop the toy at this simple command.

The "leave it" command. This command is the

act of putting a treat or something else the dog wants in close proximity to them and instructing them to "leave it" or to not eat or touch it. You teach them to it by getting two treats and holding one in each hand. Hide one in one hand and show the dog the treat in the other. Put it right in front of their face and let them smell or lick at it. Once they realize you're not going to let go or give them the treat, they'll usually back off and might growl a little. When they do this, say "leave it." Once they're still, give them the treat in the other hand. Do this over and over again until they can obey the command without you having to wait. Once they can do this, try throwing a treat on the ground and see if they obey the command then.

The "bed" command. This command is the simple act of getting your Lab to go over to its bed. To teach them this trick, you'll need a treat and a leash. Hook them onto the leash and put a treat in your other hand. Direct your dog over to their bed (or where ever they sleep) with both the treat and the leash. Once your Lab gets there, say "bed" and give them a treat. Try this over and over again until you don't have to guide them with the leash, then try it without the treat. It should get to the point where they'll go over to their bed by the simple command. This will make it easy to get your dog in bed for the night.

The "stand up" command. This command is commanding your dog to stand on its hind legs and butt. Before you teach them this, they need to know the "sit" command. It's taught using a treat. You command the Lab to sit and then hold a treat out over their head. They'll reach for it higher and higher until they're forced to stand on their hind legs. When they do this, give them the treat and say "stand up."

The "no" command. This is an important

command for your dog to know. If it's doing something it shouldn't or going somewhere it shouldn't or anything like that, this can help your dog turn its attention back to you and stop whatever might happen. To teach this, you need a leash and a treat. You place the treat on the ground, put your Lab on the leash, and slowly walk your Lab over towards it. When the treat gets your Lab's attention and it goes to eat it, pull back softly on the leash and say "no." Then give them a treat. Do this over and over again until they back away from the treat without you having to pull back. Then try it without a leash.

The "calm down" command. This is a good command for your dog to know which you can use when your dog gets overly-excited. Its purpose is to get your dog to hold still and calm down. To teach them this trick, you need a treat and a leash. Using the leash, lead your dog to a couch or other soft area. Get them to lie down in the area and then say "settle down" and give them a treat. Then direct them back up and lead them right outside the area and say "okay" and give them another treat. Do this until you don't have to guide them when you say either command.

The "heel" command. This is a good command for your dog to know when going for walks. If your Lab gets really good at it, it could even be the first step to not having to use a leash on a walk. Basically, it's just the command that tells your dog it's supposed to be walking or standing right to the side of your legs, its front legs parallel with yours. You'll need a leash and a treat. You can tie the leash into your belt loop, making your dog unable to walk anywhere other than beside you but not too tight it's uncomfortable for them. Then try walking with them. Every time your Lab pulls on the leash, go in the opposite direction as they are pulling.

When the leash becomes loose, say "heel" and give them a treat. Do this over and over again until they can "heel" at command. Then try it without a leash.

New Games

Exotic fetching. Throwing the same ball every time you play fetch with your dog can get a little boring. Keep yourself and your Lab interested in the game by getting some different things to play fetch with. Try stuffed animals or other types of toys. You can also try throwing things that might be a little difficult for your dog to pick up and bring back to you.

Frisbee. Frisbee is one of the most beloved dog games. To play this game, your dog should already know how to fetch. What's good about Frisbee in the fact that the object doesn't fall right to the ground. Instead, it hovers in the air and moves much slower than a regular ball. If your dog's fast enough, which they probably are, they can run and catch up to it. If you do this enough and your dog gets really good, they can even catch it in the air. Not only is this game fun, as you get to throw a Frisbee, you also get the immense pleasure of watching your dog catch a Frisbee in the air. It's also very impressive to strangers.

Fight the Water. You've probably seen videos online of dogs going crazy trying to bite the stream of water shooting out of hoses. Well, if you didn't know, Labs love water. All you need to play this game is a yard, a hose, and a water source. Simply point the house slightly up into the air, maybe spraying your dog at first to get their attention. Soon they'll be jumping up at it and going crazy. A big benefit of this game is that, while it makes your dog go crazy and expend a bunch of energy, all you have to do is hold the hose. So this is a good game for you to play with your dog when it's just one of those days where you're just too tired to do much else.

The Chase. Dogs are predators. Few things can get dogs as excited as chasing a squirrel or other wild animal. Well, this is a way to play into that part of your Lab without anything having to die. How you play this game is by getting a stuffed animal and tying it to a long rope. Get your Lab interested in it and then pull it away from them as fast as you can. They'll run after it and try to catch it. When it gets back to you, throw it out and repeat the process.

Soccer. A fun game to play with your dog is to get a soccer ball, which is probably a bigger object than your dog can fit in its mouth, and kick it around. They'll run after the ball and go crazy. You can just keep kicking it and watch them chase after it. They'll try to bite is and it'll just get further away from them. Very funny to watch!

Flirt Pole. A Flirt Pole is a long stick with a lure at the end of it. You tease your dog with the lure and then watch as it chases it around. It's a really good game when you don't feel like doing much because all you have to do is move the stick and watch the dog wear itself out. When you're playing this, make sure to tone it down from time to time. This can really tire dogs out as they make sharp turns and sprint to catch the lure. You should also be sure to let your dog catch the lure every once in a while to keep their interest.

Bubbles. This is another game where you don't have to do much. All you need is some soapy water and a bubble blower. Get your Lab near you and blow some bubbles. Now watch as it goes crazy trying to get them. Just keep blowing bubbles around them and they'll entertain themselves. It's also fun to watch the bubbles pop on your Lab's nose!

Find the Treat. The last game we'll cover is a simple game of hiding one of your dog's favorite treats. Have them sit in another room or on the other side of a big room. Then hide the treat on the floor or on a short counter. Then release them from their place and watch as they look furiously for the treat. You can play this on days when you can go outside and it doesn't require much exercise on your part.

Conclusion

There's a reason Labrador Retrievers are the most popular dogs in the United States. They are smart dogs that get along well with both children and other dogs. A Labrador Retriever brings people together and completes a family because they are part of the family. For thousands of years, dogs and humans have shared the same living spaces and enjoyed each other's company. Having a dog in your life can be the difference between a home that is empty, quiet, and lonely to a home that is vibrant, warm, and loving. Dogs serve as a faithful companion that is always loving and accepting, no matter who you are or what you do.

However, there is a difference between having a Labrador Retriever that's not trained and having a Labrador Retriever that's well trained. Having a well-trained Labrador Retriever opens up your options. You can go more places, meet more dogs, and meet more people. You can take them to huge parks in the country and let them run around off their leash without having to worry about them running away and getting into trouble because they'll always come back to you and they'll always respond to your commands. Being well-trained is also a huge benefit to the Labrador itself. They get challenges. They feel as though they have a purpose. They have little jobs to do, and dogs love having jobs to do. Well-trained Labs also have an incredibly fulfilling relationship with their owners. The bond an owner gets with their dog in the process of training is one of the closest bonds any one person can have with a dog. A well-trained dog can also go anywhere dogs can go. The owner never has to worry about their well-trained Lab because that Lab understands the world and the importance of order in ways that other, non-trained dogs simply don't.

It's also very beneficial to the dog owner to have a well-trained dog. It opens up your options as to where you can go with your dog and what you can do. It makes sure that the time you spend with your dog will never be boring and you won't ever feel like your dog isn't getting enough attention and you'll never be afraid that they aren't happy. It's also really good if you have children. Having a well-trained Lab is a very good thing to have around children because it will teach them how to not be afraid of dogs as well as how to treat them and raise a healthy, well-trained dog.

It's also a load of fun to train your Lab. While simply playing with your dog might get old after a while, the process of teaching a dog all the commands you can is very different. You put in the time and you never feel as if you're wasting it. At the end of every day during the training process, you see a change in your dog. It listens to you a little better. It looks at you for more cues than before. It can read your mood better. It trusts you more and is more comfortable around you. You also get to see them doing things they couldn't do before. You get to watch your Lab grow like a child. They learn new skills. They get better, faster, and stronger. You get to impress people with how well your dog is trained and you come across as a put-together, orderly person.

You also won't ever have to worry about your dog when people come over or when the two of you go somewhere. You can take it to the dog park and be relaxed and open the whole time. You don't have to worry about waking up to messes. You don't have to worry about your dog getting off its leash somehow and not being able to get a hold of it. You don't have to worry that your dog will bark all night and annoy the neighbors.

Training your dog can improve every part of its life. Well-trained dogs are far less likely to be given up for adoption than dogs that aren't trained. They're far less likely to be put down or attacked by other dogs. You don't need to fear that your dog will attack a child or kill another dog. Your dog will be calm and passive and under control as long as you're there to give it a command.

We've covered a lot of topics in this book. I hope that you found it helpful and that you learned a lot. I hope your training goes well, and please remember that it never hurts to come back to this to refresh your knowledge, or to solve problems that may arise.

About The Author

Kimberly Lawrence is a lifelong animal lover, artist and writer. Her entire career centers around animals, mainly dogs. She has owned Labs, collies, shelties, mixed breeds, and dachshunds, while fostering dozens of different breeds for rescue organizations over the years. She worked several years as a dog trainer, doing private training and classes at a board-and-train facility in San Francisco. Since then, She has been pet sitting and boarding dogs in her home for over 10 years.

Kimberly now live in Southern California with a Lab, a dachshund and two rescued cats. When not writing or walking with her dogs, Kimberly enjoys spending time horseback riding with her daughters or relaxing at the lake with her husband. She always has an assortment of guest dogs to keep her busy.